**BOOKS BY WILLIAM POUNDSTONE**

BIG SECRETS
THE RECURSIVE UNIVERSE
BIGGER SECRETS
LABYRINTHS OF REASON

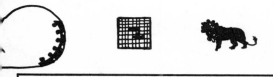

# THE ULTIMATE

T      H      E

# ULTIMATE

# WILLIAM POUNDSTONE

DOUBLEDAY · NEW YORK   LONDON   TORONTO   SYDNEY   AUCKLAND

PUBLISHED BY DOUBLEDAY
a division of Bantam Doubleday Dell Publishing Group, Inc.
666 Fifth Avenue, New York, New York 10103

DOUBLEDAY and the portrayal of an anchor
with a dolphin are trademarks of Doubleday,
a division of Bantam Doubleday Dell
Publishing Group, Inc.

DESIGNED BY BONNI LEON
ILLUSTRATED BY MARTIN BERMAN

Library of Congress Cataloging-in-Publication Data

Poundstone, William.
The ultimate / William Poundstone. — 1st ed.
p.   cm.
1. Handbooks, vade-mecums, etc. 2. Curiosities and wonders.
3. World records.   I. Title.
AG105.P78   1990

031.02—dc20                                                    90-30685
                                                                        CIP

ISBN 0-385-24260-3

TO WALTER GARDNER

## ACKNOWLEDGMENTS

I am indebted to all those who suggested lines of research, provided information or contacts, or served on comparison panels. The analyses in the sports chapters draw heavily on statistics kept by professional organizations and dedicated fans over the years. Special thanks go to Nancy V. Gauss, Russell R. Grundke, William Hilliard, Lawrence Hussar, Gale E. Johnson, Brian Leibowitz, Ruth Letowsky, Linda Litchfield, Sue Mitschke, Julia Morton, John Novak, James E. Pennington, D.D.S., Kathy Poundstone, William Poundstone, Sr., the staff of the Professional Golfers' Association, Art Rilling, Doel Soejarto, Surachai Wattanaporn, and K. G. Whitford.

# CONTENTS

T H E
# ULTIMATE

# INTRODUCTION

America likes superlatives. The biggest! The best! The most! Something in the national character insists that value judgments can be democratized and mechanized, put to a vote and settled. It's how we determine our President. It's how we determine our Miss America. See the world's biggest pony and the world's smallest pony, and you have a pretty good handle on the pony situation.

The world is a more orderly place when things can be compared and ranked. Or *would* be if people agreed. The ultimate-watcher quickly discovers that many contradictory claims exist. How many sports figures are claimed to be "the best of all time"? How many buildings are the tallest? How many foods are the most delicious? The answer is: "A lot," going by the pronouncements of experts and amateurs alike.

You can't very well expect to settle something like what's the best sports car or the most livable American city. The answer depends too heavily on what attributes one thinks are important in sports cars or cities. All you can say is that you share someone's tastes or you don't. There are therefore two approaches to this business of superlatives. The perennial "bests" and "worsts" lists and books admit the subjectivity of such comparisons. They are based on personal opinion, usually that of an expert whose opinion carries some weight. In such cases the opinion says as much about the tastes of the expert as about the matter in question. That may be interesting in itself. It is not likely to convince someone holding the opposite opinion—nor, perhaps, is it intended to do so.

This book focuses on another type of superlative. There is a hardest hole of golf, a scariest amusement park ride, and a most difficult tongue twister. Sure, people may argue about these things. That's because no one goes to the trouble of comparing golf holes, rides, or tongue twisters, at least not in any methodical sense. The fact remains that some hole of golf causes more players to lose games than any other (as revealed in official records of tournament play), some ride subjects passengers to the greatest disorienting force (as calculated from height and angle of drop), and some tongue twister causes more people to stumble than any other (as revealed in tests with people asked to read a list of hard tongue twisters). These types of superlatives involve value judgments—they are not pat enough to be listed in the *Guinness Book of World Records*—but they are not purely matters of taste. The superlatives can be revealed through research, and once revealed, most reasonable people can agree on them.

Everyone likes to win an argument. Here, then, is your chance. There are two sides to every dispute, and that means someone is wrong. Plain, bozo-brained wrong. Our researchers set out to expose those people publicly. No longer will you have to endure the interminable debates of polite society: Whether Babe Ruth was the best baseball player of all time. The most profitable form of investment. Whether beluga caviar deserves its reputation. *We've settled the matter once and for all.* In the midst of unbridled opinion—before friends who only think they know what they're talking about—here are the facts.

# THE
# HARDEST
# HOLE
# OF GOLF

# JACK
# NICKLAUS CALLED

Augusta National's 12th hole "the most demanding tournament hole in the world." Strangely, Nicklaus has won the Masters Tournament, playing this very hole, six times. "I consider it the most dangerous hole in golf," confided Cary Middlecoff about the same killer 12th, but it didn't prevent Middlecoff from winning a Masters Tournament either. Fellow Masters winners Arnold Palmer, Sam Snead, and Gary Player were almost as emphatic in declaring the 12th hole—"Golden Bell" on Augusta's botanical card—the toughest par-3 in golf. Possibly a more authoritative opinion on the awfulness of the 12th would come from nonwinner Tom Weiskopf, who took 13 strokes on it during the 1980 Masters Tournament. That was the worst ever in tournament play. If Weiskopf expressed an opinion on the hole, it has not been recorded.

You can find similar opinions on dozens of holes nationwide, with the pros most willing to expound on the difficulty of holes they have just done well on. "Absolutely the toughest," was how Ben Crenshaw described the 18th hole on Doral's Blue Monster course (Miami) for *USA Today* after winning the 1988 Doral Ryder Open. Raymond Floyd called the 18th "the toughest par four in the world. I've had sixes and sevens on it hundreds of times." Floyd made this admission of vulnerability after winning the Doral Ryder Open twice. Ben Hogan called the 15th at Oakmont Country Club (near Pittsburgh) the most demanding he ever played, and you'd be wrong if you thought this was the scene of some sort of golf Waterloo for him.

It's not just the players who disagree. Sportswriter Angus G. Garber III claimed the 16th hole on Firestone Country Club's south course (Akron, Ohio) was the hardest: "They don't come any tougher than this one," he writes in *Golf Legends* (1988). The Professional Golfers' Association "officially" rates the 16th hole at Cypress Point (Pebble Beach, Calif.) as the hardest on the PGA tour. The other bastion of pro golfdom, the U.S. Golf Association, rates courses rather than individual holes. It claims that PGA West's Stadium course (La Quinta, Calif.) is the hardest in the country.

Everyone who plays golf talks about how hard holes are. The average player has limited experience of holes and courses, but you might hope that the pros and sportswriters, who know the game and the top courses the best, would be able to come to a consensus. Is there any way of deciding, once and for all, which hole is the hardest?

Difficult holes don't just happen. More than one course has been designed with the express purpose of being the hardest in the world. That was the goal of George Crump, who designed most of Clementon, N.J.,'s storied Pine Valley beginning in 1912. Crump did not live to see the course's completion in 1922. Charles Price called it "one big 200-acre, unraked bunker." One sand trap, "Hell's Half-Acre," is said to be the largest in the world.

Pine Valley retains its reputation as a tough course, but several generations of newer courses are snapping at its heels. Today there is a flourishing cult of the difficult in golf-course design. Nearly every course that architect Pete Dye designs is lauded as tougher than anything he's done before, the toughest in the world. Dye's PGA West is so difficult that many of the pros signed a petition to have it taken off the Bob Hope–Chrysler Classic rotation. To many, this only enhanced the cachet of playing there: 45,000 rounds a year of amateur golf are played at PGA West, with greens fees of $125.

It stands to reason that differences in difficulty should be reflected in players' scores. Not all courses keep scoring statistics on their holes. Even when they do, the statistics are not directly comparable with those from other courses. The "average" player at a private course with a jock reputation is usually more accomplished than the "average" player at a municipal course.

The most practical way of comparing courses is through scoring in professional tournament play. The pro tours send a fairly consistent group of excellent players to many, though not all, of the finest and presumably hardest courses in the country. Statistics on tournament play are readily available from the governing bodies of golf.

What exactly is a difficult hole of golf? Well, sure, it has something to do with sand traps and water. "Hardness" of a golf hole is subtler than it first appears. You win by getting the lowest score. So maybe a hard hole is one that takes a lot of strokes. Figure the average number of strokes taken on each hole, and the hole with the highest average should be the hardest.

In the years 1983–85, the PGA tour covered 46 courses. Out of those 828 PGA holes, the ten that required the most strokes, on the average, were as follows:

| Course | Hole | Par | Average Strokes |
|--------|------|-----|-----------------|
| Pebble Beach | 14 | 5 | 5.172 |
| Spyglass Hill | 1 | 5 | 5.158 |
| Pebble Beach | 18 | 5 | 5.140 |
| Butler National | 7 | 5 | 5.118 |
| La Costa | 17 | 5 | 5.086 |
| Butler National | 15 | 5 | 5.067 |
| Desert Inn | 5 | 5 | 5.065 |
| TPC at Sawgrass | 9 | 5 | 5.058 |
| Doral (Blue) | 12 | 5 | 5.020 |
| Glen Abbey | 13 | 5 | 5.009 |

This doesn't mean much. *All* the above holes are par-5s. They would almost have to be. A par-5 is supposed to require more strokes than a par-4 or a par-3.

No one seems to have ever mentioned the 14th at Pebble Beach as the hardest hole in golf—or even the hardest hole at Pebble Beach. It's a nice par-5 on a tough course, that's all. Nor does anyone consider par-5s tougher, as a class, than par-4s and par-3s. If anything, the opposite: Bobby Jones complained that "you don't start playing golf until the third shot" on most par-5s.

If average strokes measured difficulty, the toughest holes of golf would be those rare holes of par 6 or greater. There are no par-6s on the PGA tour. There is a par-7 hole (of 909 yards) on the Sano course of the Satsuki Golf Club in Japan. Then there is an 830-yard hole of par 7.5 at the Hammersley Hills Golf Club (Pawling, N.Y.), the personal course at the estate of film producer Dino De Laurentiis. Designer Robert Trent Jones indulged a whim to have decimal pars.

This isn't what anyone means by a tough hole. An easy hole may simply be long enough to require 5, 6, or more strokes. Length alone doesn't make a hole hard.

Perhaps difficulty has more to do with stroke "density": strokes *per yard*. Take the average number of strokes and divide it by the hole's length. The higher the result, the more difficult the hole.

Since most championship courses have a par around 70 and a total distance of about 7,000 yards, the average stroke density is very nearly 1 stroke per 100 yards. Freak long holes like those just mentioned usually have a low stroke density. By stroke density, the ten toughest holes on the PGA tour go like this:

| Course | Hole | Par | Average | Length | Strokes per 100 Yards |
|---|---|---|---|---|---|
| Pebble Beach | 7 | 3 | 3.070 | 107 | 2.869 |
| TPC at Sawgrass | 17 | 3 | 3.174 | 132 | 2.405 |
| Spyglass Hill | 15 | 3 | 3.014 | 130 | 2.318 |
| Glen Abbey | 15 | 3 | 3.060 | 141 | 2.170 |
| Cypress Point | 15 | 3 | 2.966 | 139 | 2.134 |
| Westchester | 6 | 3 | 2.827 | 133 | 2.126 |
| Augusta National | 12 | 3 | 3.261 | 155 | 2.104 |
| Spyglass Hill | 3 | 3 | 3.108 | 150 | 2.072 |
| Westchester | 14 | 3 | 2.946 | 144 | 2.046 |
| Glen Abbey | 3 | 3 | 3.170 | 156 | 2.032 |

(Some holes are so close that the exact rank may vary from year to year. An unseasonable wind can scramble the rankings for that year. Similar caveats apply to most of the following discussion.)

The top-rated hole, by a significant margin, is the 7th at Pebble Beach. This hole, the shortest on the PGA tour, is indeed renowned as a tough one. It is on the tip of a peninsula jutting into the ocean. Usually players drive straight into strong sea breezes. The wind was so bad one year that Sam Snead putted his way from tee to hole on the dirt path to the green.

Second is the spectacular island-green 17th hole of TPC at

Sawgrass. Seventh on the list is Augusta's notorious 12th, the terror of Amen Corner and frequently on pros' lists of hardest holes. All the holes above are considered difficult *short* holes.

They're all par-3s. The criterion of stroke density favors "heroic" holes with a single, obvious hazard, like a lake between tee and green. It downgrades holes that are merely long but not otherwise difficult.

For a par-4 or par-5 to attain a high stroke density, it would have to be an obstacle course, with stroke-robbing hazards all along the way. No actual PGA hole is quite that brutal. The stroke-density criterion emphasizes putting because you are apt to spend a couple of strokes negotiating the last few yards to the hole. Holes with fast or undulating greens ought to have particularly high stroke densities.

The emphasis on putting is so acute that, in terms of stroke density, almost any miniature golf course hole is more "difficult" than the toughest real golf holes. A typical miniature golf course has a par of 54 and a total distance of about 300 yards. That means that the average miniature golf hole has a density of about 18 par strokes per 100 yards. For a real tricked-up item (hit the ball in the alligator's mouth and it comes out his tail) it could be 40 or more.

Miniature golf isn't categorically "harder" than real golf by most people's standards. Stroke density isn't the whole story on difficulty.

You're probably way ahead of me. When golfers talk about hard holes, they're usually thinking of the difficulty of making par. You often play against par as much as against your partners.

Good players (and TV commentators) measure performance against par. Hence terms like "bogey" and "birdie."

The par is somewhat arbitrary. You might expect that from its circuitous definition. Par is what a scratch golfer would shoot, on the average, and a scratch golfer is someone who shoots par.

The USGA has distance recommendations for assigning pars. A hole of up to 250 yards is usually a par-3 for men; par-4s normally run up to 470 yards; par-5s are anything longer. Ultimately, the par is decided at the caprices of the course architect and the club management.

As most golfers reflect at one time or another, the par is not always fair. The 16th at Cypress Point (233 yards) is a par-3 that, almost everyone thinks, ought to be a par-4. The 18th at Harbour Town (Hilton Head, S.C.; 465 yards) is a 4 that could be a 5. Both comply with the USGA distance guidelines. They're just difficult for their length.

Even if such flukes were ironed out, there would still be the round-off error that concerned Robert Trent Jones: What if a hole is really a par-4.5? Barring fractional pars, there is a range of difficulties in any par class. The holes listed as par-4 on the card must actually range from theoretical par-3.5 through par-4.5—plus a few errant values outside the range.

Try this third definition of difficulty: The toughest hole is the one most underrated by its par. This is the definition adopted by the PGA when it lists the "toughest" holes on the tour in its annual media guide. If you measure your score against par and know that a par-4 that should be a par-5 is coming up, you can expect to lose a stroke, relative to par. It is a "hard" hole because it costs you an extra stroke.

On the U.S. pro tour, the most difficult hole relative to par is (rather dependably) the par-3 16th hole at Cypress Point. Touring professionals have averaged about 3.6 strokes. (It's anyone's guess what a regular player would average.) The list of top ten holes for 1983–85 runs:

| Course | Hole | Par | Average | Average Minus Par |
|---|---|---|---|---|
| Cypress Point | 16 | 3 | 3.636 | 0.636 |
| Westchester | 12 | 4 | 4.516 | 0.516 |
| Bay Hill | 18 | 4 | 4.510 | 0.510 |
| Spyglass Hill | 8 | 4 | 4.441 | 0.441 |
| Desert Inn | 7 | 3 | 3.435 | 0.435 |
| TPC at Sawgrass | 18 | 4 | 4.435 | 0.435 |
| Cypress Point | 14 | 4 | 4.431 | 0.431 |
| Glen Abbey | 14 | 4 | 4.420 | 0.420 |
| Doral (Blue) | 18 | 4 | 4.407 | 0.407 |
| Cypress Point | 8 | 4 | 4.401 | 0.401 |

Most of these ten are widely regarded as difficult holes, though to different degrees. The most notorious ones, other than Cypress Point's 16th, are probably the 18th at TPC at Sawgrass (Ponte Vedra Beach, Fla.) and Raymond Floyd's alleged nemesis, the 18th at Doral.

More thought calls this criterion into question, too. What it really boils down to is an unfair par. That is trivial and unsatisfying. Par is nothing more than a handy bit of free information offered players. The game could exist without it. If an understated par was all there is to a challenging hole, then *any* hole could become the hardest in the world by reassigning its par as one.

What if Cypress Point's management finally gave in and changed the par to 4? Then the hole's statistical hardness would vanish like a hook shot into gorse. What if we abolished pars altogether? Wouldn't some holes still be harder than others?

If Cypress Point's 16th is merely the case of a par-3 that should be a par-4, it shouldn't pose any great dread for closely matched players approaching it. No one loses a game because of a misleading par. All players play the same hole with the same trick par.

Ultimately, you do play golf against the other players. A hole that is in some sense "hard"—but equally "hard" for all—cannot make a difference in the game's outcome. You might ask, *is* there such a thing as a hard hole of golf? A hard hole is one that causes someone to *lose.* A hole can't hurt your score unless it is possible (perhaps likely) that you will take more strokes than your partners. The holes you have to worry about are ones that magnify differences of ability, judgment, and luck.

A difficult hole discriminates. It may simply be a crapshoot that punishes the unlucky. More likely, it punishes those who can't hit far enough, can't aim well enough, or try to do something stupid. The better player stays on the fairway, while the worse player ends up in sand traps, high grass, trees, rocks, cactus, or water. A difficult hole allows, even tempts, the mediocre player to make a *self-perpetuating fatal error.*

In the small but competitive world of course architecture,

this concept goes by the name of *penal* design. The Platonic ideal of a penal hole would be one where either you get a hole in one or it's totally hopeless—like those joke paintings of impossible holes straddling the Grand Canyon or perched on an ice floe. More practically, a penal hole is one where a poor player (or a good player who has made a bad shot) takes as many extra strokes as possible, relative to a good or lucky player. A penal hole maximizes the embarrassment of the duffer.

Penal architecture has been in and out of fashion several times. The original Scottish courses evolved over many years on links land, a hilly seaside waste. By American standards, most Scottish courses are highly penal. Sand is everywhere, roughs are untended, and winds are strong and variable. The player who fails to drive accurately is apt to have a much more difficult second shot.

Many feel that the game of golf was greatly improved by the more parklike courses built in the United States and elsewhere in the early part of the century. Lacking natural links land, Americans bulldozed and landscaped course sites into prefabricated paradises. Fairways were synthetic, distended glades, and sand traps were shallow, cosmetic props. Bad shots could still land safely on a manicured fairway and afford a good lie.

Course architect Robert Trent Jones theorized that "every hole should be a hard par and an easy bogey." He felt that "the first purpose of any golf course should be to give pleasure, and that to the greatest number of players . . . because it will offer problems a man may attempt according to his ability. It will never become hopeless for the duffer nor fail to concern and interest the expert . . ."

Jones's populist manifesto is well taken. Why make the duffer dig himself into a sand trap and take three strokes to get out? Does the weekend golfer enjoy that?

More to the point, all but the wealthiest, most exclusive of courses have to be concerned about throughput. A course that makes players take more strokes takes longer to play. Easier courses permit more greens fees and more dues-paying members. Anyway, most flashy new courses are built to sell real estate. The assumption is that course-side houses and condominiums sell to people who have made their money at something other than golf and are not yearning to be humiliated with exceptional challenges. Developers try to please everyone with a course that is attractive and not too hard.

In recent decades penal design has staged a comeback. The best-known modern exponent is Pete Dye. Those who hire him to design a course generally want the notoriety of a super-hard course. The developers of PGA West's Stadium course told Dye to "make it tougher than Oak Tree, tougher than TPC, tougher than anything in the country." They pridefully claim that more golf balls are lost there than anywhere else in the country. There are many ways of making a course punishing. Dye is known for "English muffin" mounds (as at La Quinta) and railroad ties or telephone poles. A typical Dye course uses up to 8,000 ties (about a mile's worth of track). Dye has brought back the controversial "blind hole" of old Scottish courses, where you cannot see the tee from the green.

Suppose we say that a tough hole is one that penalizes poor or unlucky shots. There are several conceivable ways of measuring the discriminating quality of a hole.

One might be the difference in score between an "average" player and a professional. Few clubs have any record of what the average player scores on particular holes, and the level of skill varies from club to club. Direct comparison between average members' scores and pros' scores is complicated by the fact that tees are moved back for tournament play.

The tournament statistics alone give a good idea of how penal a hole is. On acutely penal holes, even the pros' scores vary greatly. Take the average score of tournament pros on a given hole, and then take the average amount by which the pros' scores vary from that average. This is what statisticians call a *mean deviation.*

If, say, everyone shoots par, then the mean deviation is zero. That's because the average score is par, and everyone has done precisely average—there is no deviation from average. When scores are spread out, with lots of birdies, bogeys, eagles, and double bogeys, the mean deviation is high. The mean deviation essentially measures how spread out the scores are. A high mean deviation means that some players are doing better than others.

The statistics are for the touring pros, but they probably give a good picture of the relative difficulty of holes for more average players, too. The top ten holes by mean deviation are:

| Course | Hole | Par | Average | Mean Deviation* |
|---|---|---|---|---|
| Cypress Point | 16 | 3 | 3.636 | 0.778 |
| Cypress Point | 8 | 4 | 4.401 | 0.766 |
| Bay Hill | 18 | 4 | 4.510 | 0.732 |
| Cypress Point | 9 | 4 | 4.197 | 0.714 |
| TPC at Sawgrass | 18 | 4 | 4.435 | 0.691 |

| Course | Hole | Par | Average | Mean Deviation* |
|--------|------|-----|---------|-----------------|
| Doral (Blue) | 18 | 4 | 4.407 | 0.679 |
| Cypress Point | 14 | 4 | 4.431 | 0.677 |
| Butler National | 14 | 4 | 4.339 | 0.676 |
| Las Vegas | 18 | 5 | 4.832 | 0.675 |
| Butler National | 10 | 4 | 4.373 | 0.670 |

* Note for the statistically minded: I used mean rather than standard deviation mainly because it is simpler to explain. Using standard deviation would change the rankings (although not radically, considering that these are the top ten out of 828 holes). The 9th at Cypress Point has the highest standard deviation. Second is the 8th at Cypress Point, and third is the 16th.

This is the only criterion of difficulty that appears to put holes of different par on an equal footing. The top ten includes a par-3 of 233 yards as well as a par-5 of 524 yards. Most of the top ten are par-4s, which is what most holes are.

Four of the ten hardest holes are at Cypress Point! The most difficult hole by mean deviation is again the 16th hole at Cypress Point. This is a rather remarkable coincidence. There is no particular reason for the hole with the highest mean deviation also to be the hole hardest relative to par. One hole on the list above, the 18th at Las Vegas Country Club, averages *less* than its par.

Besides having an unrealistically low par, the 16th at Cypress Point is a classic penal hole. It does respectably well by the stroke-density criterion, too, averaging 1.561 strokes per 100 yards (about 133rd out of 828 PGA holes). That makes Cypress Point's 16th the hardest hole on the PGA tour.

Is it the hardest hole in the country? In the world? Few dispute that most of the hardest courses are on the pro tour. There's no reason to build and maintain a killer course just for attorneys and investment bankers on their day off. A few hard courses are not on the PGA tour, though. Oakmont isn't, and neither is Pine Valley. Neither has the wind that is so much a factor at Cypress Point, and it is doubtful that any of their holes are quite as penal.

Many of the old British courses are renowned for their difficulty. On the basis of the scorecards for the 1987 British Open played at Muirfield, the hole with the greatest mean deviation was the 4th. It had a mean deviation of 0.649 strokes, which would not have made the top ten list of PGA holes.

What makes Cypress Point's 16th so hard? The Cypress Point Golf Club was designed in 1928 by Alister Mackenzie and Robert Hunter, a pair of go-to-hell iconoclasts who dared to put two par-5s and two par-3s back to back. (The 16th hole is the second of the pair of 3s.) Cypress Point is one of the least-used courses in the country. Deer and elk stroll deserted fairways in morning and late afternoon. The club has only 240 members, most of them captains of industry or celebrities who live somewhere other than the Monterey Peninsula. Bob Hope, who is a member, quipped, "One year we had a big membership drive—and drove out fifty members." Annual dues are reportedly sky high, and no one cares.

No townies are allowed, even during the AT&T Pebble Beach Pro-Am—the club's one brush with notoriety. It is almost impossible to wangle an invitation to play. ("The members al-

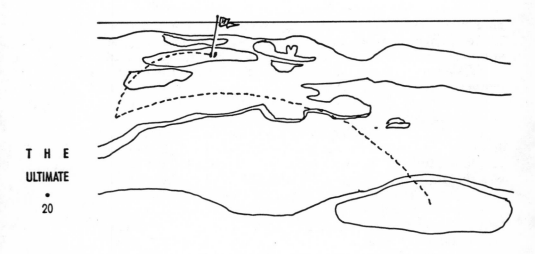

ready know everyone they want to know," according to one report.)

The 16th at Cypress Point is a much-photographed hole, well
known to TV viewers. It is the short hole that forces a drive
across ocean waves breaking against Bel Air cigarette-ad land-
scape. Achieving par requires a 220-foot carry over the Pacific.
The basic wimp strategy is a drive to the left, avoiding the water. Even some pros do this.

The principal obstacles are, in order, the wind, the water, rocks, ice plant, and sand. Unlike the serenely dependable trade winds of some tropic courses, Cypress Point's winds are variable and must be judged astutely for each drive. Fifty-mile-an-hour winds are common. That's a 9 on the Beaufort scale: "strong gale: large boughs break off trees; light objects lifted off ground; roof tiles blown off." On the 16th hole, the wind is usually *against* the first drive.

The tee is elevated, providing a daunting perspective of the ocean and the green. Players who don't quite hit far enough land on the rocks below the fairway. Recovery shots are all but impossible. Once Henry Ransom tried it, hitting three fruitless shots into the rocks. The third shot ricocheted and hit Ransom in the abdomen. "When they start hitting back at you, it's time to quit," he said. The other famous bon mot inspired by the 16th is that of Jimmy Demaret: "The only place you can drop the ball over your shoulder is in Honolulu."

Players who just clear the rocks may land in ice plant, a nasty ground cover that eats golf balls. By all accounts, ice plant is much worse than sand. Every year, several star players get stuck in it, and sportscasters resort to colorful metaphors in explaining it to the folks at home. ("Like hitting from a pile of gherkins" is a good one.) Four sand traps cluster around the green.

Horror stories: Scores of up to 10 among *professional* golfers are too numerous to mention. At the 1953 Crosby tournament, Ed (Porky) Oliver, a contender for the championship, took 16 strokes. This included an unbroken series of five shots into the sea and a protracted battle with the ice plant. Oliver did not win the tournament. In 1959 Hans Merrell, another pro, took 19 strokes—a rare *sexdecuple* bogey.

What makes the 16th infuriating is that other people luck out. Bing Crosby shot a hole in one in 1947.

# THE
# TOUGHEST
# SHOT IN
# BILLIARDS

# SOMETIME IN THE 1890S

the Belgian expert Professor Kaarless made a spectacular draw shot that was acclaimed the greatest shot ever made in the game of billiards. The red ball was frozen flush against one side of the table. The white object ball was near a corner on the far side. The cue ball was almost diagonally opposite it. Kaarless hit the cue ball with draw and English. It hit the red ball, caromed back onto the cushion, returned to hit two rails and finally hit the other white ball.

Billiards' appeal rests in the fact that every shot is different. However, artistic billiards tournaments pit players against seventy-six of the game's hardest shots, exactingly set up with templates. Kaarless's miracle shot is now part of the *standard* tournament repertoire. In artistic tournaments, each player is allotted three tries to make a shot. Making a shot is worth 4 to 11 points depending on difficulty. Just four shots are worth the maximum of 11 points. They are the three-cushion draw (Kaarless's shot, slightly modified), the four-cushion draw, the five-cushion massé, and the direct carom massé with imposed limit.

Of the four, the five-cushion massé is the most complex and possibly the most challenging. The two draw shots involve fewer rebounds. The direct carom massé requires the cue ball to make a mind-bending 90-degree turn around an obstacle placed on the table, but there are no rebounds to worry about.

The five-cushion massé looks flatly impossible:

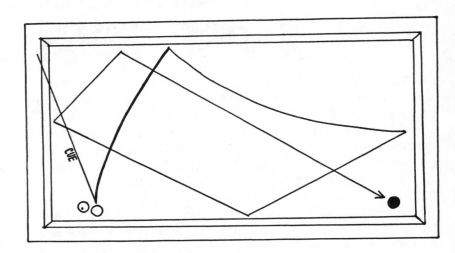

FIVE-CUSHION MASSÉ SHOT

The white object ball and the cue ball are near the first diamond on one long side of the table (call it south). The red ball is near the southeast corner. The cue is held almost vertically for a massé stroke. The dotted line shows how to aim. Think of it as the shadow that would be cast by the cue stick at high noon.

Massé shots always threaten to rip the cloth and smash the table. This has to be a jackhammer-force shot. Relatively little of a massé stroke's energy goes into horizontal motion, and the ball has to hit five rails. The massé shot draws the cue ball backward, just enough to smack into the white ball and rebound onto the north rail. It has considerable spin, giving it an arcing path on the first two rebounds. Then it hits the east rail, the south rail, the west rail, and again the north rail. On its last rebound, it travels nearly the full diagonal length of the table to hit the red ball.

"Forget it," says Robert Byrne of this shot in his *Treasury of Trick Shots in Pool and Billiards* (1982). There are several reasons why this is the hardest shot in billiards.

It's a massé shot, which is difficult to begin with.

It's an extremely long shot. The longer the shot, the more accurately it must be aimed. The margin for error in a six-foot shot is clearly less than in a one-foot shot. The tolerance is finer yet in a shot that, because of rebounds, is longer than the table. The total distance traveled in the five-rail massé is about 3 1/2 times the long side of the table, or 28 times the distance between the diamonds, or (on a full-size table) 35 feet. Suppose you can calculate the angles with perfect confidence. Five rebounds is nothing; to you it's all the same as one straight shot folded up. Even then, the five-rail massé would be like hitting the red ball from 35 feet away on a giant table. In Kaarless's shot, the distance is a bit over two sides, or 23 feet.

That a shot this long is possible at all is due to the "big ball" effect. The red ball's corner placement permits a maximal margin of error on the final leg of the ball's travel. All the cue ball has to do is touch the red ball. Whether it hits dead center or just kisses on one side or the other is all the same. Furthermore, with the red ball in the corner, the cue ball can miss it entirely, go into the cushion, and hit the red ball on the rebound. In effect, it's as if the red ball is several times larger than it really is.

It's a truism that extremely forceful shots are less accurate. This shot is near anybody's limit of shooting strength, and for that reason will be less accurate than more typical shots.

The shot depends on English to give the ball a curved path. Exactly how curved depends on how much spin is imparted. For most players this is tougher to gauge than mere direction. Each of the five rebounds imparts slight additional English through friction with the rail. Even the state of the nap of the cloth on the rails is a factor and must be figured in as well.

Not all errors are the player's fault. No table is in perfect condition. Cloth invariably has slick parts and slow parts; the rail may be unevenly worn. The longer the ball is in contact with the table, the more table imperfections can affect its course. Here again, the extreme length of the shot works against the player. On the final rebound, momentum is fading and the ball is ever more affected by surface idiosyncrasies.

For all these reasons, the five-rail massé is extraordinarily challenging. For all practical purposes, it is possible only under tournament conditions: a clean, heated table with new cloth.

(Even though it doesn't use the corners, there's not much point in trying this shot on a pool table. The cloth on a billiard table is much smoother, and the balls are ivory rather than the usual plastic. Both differences minimize friction to allow ambitious shots such as this. Some players squirt Armorall on the balls to practice difficult shots.)

Pocket billiards shooters play around with novelty shots of their own. Most involve pocketing multiple balls in one shot. You rarely see more than a 3-in-one shot in real play. The limit is much higher in carefully staged trick shots. You're allowed to arrange the balls any way you like: How many can be pocketed in one shot?

The shot that Steve Mizerak makes in a Miller Lite commercial is an oldie known as "just showing off" in pool circles. It pockets 7 balls. That's not nearly a record. The neat thing about the just-showing-off shot is that its asymmetrical placement of balls looks natural, as if it just happened to occur. You don't immediately realize that Mizerak spent a couple of minutes painstakingly arranging the balls before the cameras started rolling.

The maximal ball-pocketing shots are symmetrical and thus contrived-looking. Trick shots with as many as 8 balls (many conveniently propped at the brink of the pockets) are often easier to make than Mizerak's 7-ball shot. It is possible for an excellent player to sink all 15 balls in one tightly composed shot. In fact, it is possible to sink 16.

A player named Bill Staton popularized (maybe invented?) the 16-ball shot. It is almost identical to a 14-ball shot that has been around the better part of a century. Staton's shot is perfectly symmetrical, with the cue ball in the center touching two object balls aimed at the middle side pockets. (Remove these two object balls and you have the older 14-ball shot.) The

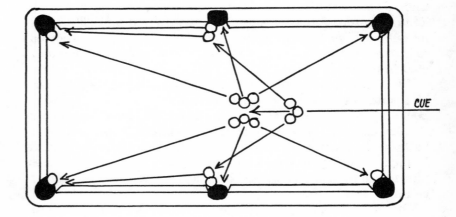

CUE

16 BALLS IN ONE SHOT

cue ball throws off these two balls and slams into a cluster of six balls, sending one to each of the six pockets.

Just so no motion is wasted, there is a ball waiting in front of each pocket—two in front of the middle pockets. The two balls at the middle pockets are touching and pointed into the pocket. The slightest touch sends the nearer ball into the pocket. The other ball goes up the table and into the corner pocket.

As in most trick shots, positioning is crucial—possibly more so than the stroke itself. The requisite stroke is forceful and perfectly centered.

Staton's shot is an optimal configuration. Improving it by adding yet more balls is more difficult than it appears. It might look like you could add another ball at each of the four corner pockets (20 balls in one shot!). If you think so, try it in miniature. Set two balls on the lip of a pocket and try to knock both in with a third object ball, *sinking the third ball as well*. The trouble is that there is no effective way of putting follow on the third ball. Notice that the two balls near the middle pockets of Staton's arrangement are sunk only by sending one of the pair into a different pocket.

# THE
# TOUGHEST
# SKI RUN

# IT'S A CINCH

telling easy runs from the tough ones at any one resort. Novice runs are posted with green circles and have names like Schoolmarm or Tinker Bell. Hard runs have double black diamonds and names like Jaws of Death, Suicide, Hangman's Hollow, and Paranoid Flat. Fergie risked her unborn baby on Méribel's (French Alps) Stairway to Hell. The trick is comparing the difficulty of runs at different resorts. What is the toughest ski run of all? Skiers being a competitive lot, this is more than a matter of idle curiosity.

The ski-resort business is competitive as well. In few other sports do facilities compete for patrons nationwide or worldwide. To attract customers, a ski area has to be the *most* of something. If it's not the closest to a nearby city, it has to be the biggest, scariest, snowiest, or longest. Vail advertises itself as the largest ski resort in North America. Jackson Hole says it has the biggest vertical drop in the United States. Whistler/

Blackcomb claims the biggest vertical drop in North America. Sun Valley advertises not only "more vertical skiing in less time than any resort in North America" but also "the largest vertical ski lift in North America." La Plagne, France, has "the longest ski lift in the world" (4 miles). Unadvertised rumors in the ski subculture allege that Alta, Utah's High Traverse, is America's most lethal slope. It has averaged a fatality every few years. The death toll may be boosted by the visibility of the run from the chair lift—skiers are tempted to show off.

The difficulty of a ski run is a matter of many factors, some of them evanescent and intangible. It is related to dimensions (how long, how steep a run is), terrain (bumpy or smooth, with or without obstructions), and snow condition.

The latter varies from day to day and hour to hour. As advertisements insist, there are general climatic differences between ski areas. New England slopes tend to be icy. Western slopes usually have drier, powdery snow. The Alps are usually somewhere in between.

It is much more difficult to control yourself on ice. Ergo, all other things being equal, an icy run is harder.

Many skiers deem the Outer Limits trail at Killington, Vt., the toughest ice skiing in the country. Located on Bear Mountain, Outer Limits has a vertical drop of 1,200 feet. It is usually pure ice. According to local folklore, a ski-shop owner once delaminated four pairs of skis in a single day. The motto of the Killington Ski School goes: "Out West you ski powder up to your knees. At Killington we teach you to ski ice up to your edges."

Another thing that makes Outer Limits difficult is moguls (snow- or ice-covered bumps). Even a beginner might snowplow down a steep even run; it is the bumps and hollows that require constant regulation and that cause most falls. Clearly moguls are another concomitant of difficulty.

What most people regard as an obstacle, some skiers actively seek out. Mach I at Peak 10, Breckenridge, Colo., site of pro mogul competitions, is considered possibly the most difficult mogul run in the country. Another difficult mogul course is the twin trails Spiral Stairs and Plunge at Telluride, Colo. Each is claimed to offer nearly a thousand turns.

Like snow condition, moguls vary with the weather. Moguls' severity depends on depth and pack of snow cover. One day they're there; the next day they're buried under new powder.

Trees are another factor contributing to difficulty. There are tree-skiing enthusiasts who enjoy the challenge of avoiding running into trees. They favor forest runs like Shadows and Twilight at Steamboat Springs, Colo. Rocks pose similar challenges.

You might imagine that the hardest runs would be obstacle courses. They'd be pure ice studded with moguls and reefs of rocks running right through a forest of trees. There *are* mountains like that, somewhere. But we're concerned with the hardest run people actually ski, and for which resort operators pay insurance premiums.

There are limits to human strength, coordination, and reaction time. The greater control possible on drier snow allows you to ski safely on slopes that are bumpier, steeper, or more obstacle-laden. Runs with trees on them aren't as steep or as bumpy, generally speaking, as bare runs in the same difficulty class. Mogul runs aren't as steep (or don't have as many trees or aren't as icy) as other runs of like caliber. If they were, people would get killed.

The dimensions of a run are the single most important factor in determining difficulty. Most skiers think it's more fun to ski on a high and steep (but relatively obstacle-free) slope than on a lesser run whose difficulty derives from avoiding obstacles. It's probably safer, too. Crashing into a tree or rock at high speed is serious. Wiping out on a too steep slope usually isn't. For that reason, the obstacle-laden slopes are mostly the province of a few specialists. The ski areas famed for expert runs—Jackson Hole, Telluride, Snowbird, Taos, and Squaw Valley—feature high, steep mountains and dry snow.

Many advertised statistics don't mean much. Vail's claim to being North America's largest ski resort refers to its land area and nothing more. The Vail complex measures 3,787 acres, or 5.9 square miles (a quarter the size of Manhattan). Jackson Hole, the biggest before Vail's expansion, has 3,000 acres. A greater area means more room and less crowding, provided that the crowds aren't proportionately bigger. A more meaningful statistic might be area per skier. Less crowded Jackson Hole would top Vail in that.

The Weissfluhjoch-Küblis Parsenn course at Davos, Switzerland, claims to be the longest alpine run in the world. It is 7.6 miles long. However, this gets into nitpicking questions of where you draw the line between Alpine and Nordic skiing. It is possible to ski down the Great Aletsch Glacier for 8 miles (promoted as the "world's longest schuss"). In fact, you can ski about 25 miles on it, though the terrain becomes virtually level. The glacier is served by a funicular and is popular, so it is a bona fide developed ski area. Is it Alpine or cross-country skiing? The vertical drop, a staggering 6,000 feet, is spread out over a 25-mile course, for a very gentle average grade of 2.6 degrees.

A long run permits greater speeds and may thereby demand greater control. A long run may test endurance. But few runs are so monumentally long that it is a big deal to complete them. Those that are, such as the long European glacier runs, grade off into the cross-country realm.

Height has more to do with difficulty. Vertical drop is the most commonly mentioned statistic, possibly because it lends itself to gross misrepresentation. This is the difference in altitude between the bottom of a run and its top—or between the bottom and top of the lift(s) serving it, which should be the same thing. One way some fudge is by measuring from the top of a mountain above the ski lift.

This makes sense only in the case of helicopter skiing areas. Alphubel, a peak reached by helicopter from Zermatt, Switzerland, has a vertical drop of 9,022 feet. The helicopter sets you down on the top of the mountain, and you ski 9,022 feet down to the base.

The Challenger lift on Sun Valley's Bald Mountain has the greatest vertical rise (3,144 feet) of any *single* lift in the U.S. as of this writing. While this is a convenience, Sun Valley's runs do not have the greatest vertical drop. Yet higher runs are served by more than one lift.

Whistler/Blackcomb Mountain in British Columbia is claimed to have the longest vertical drop of any resort in Canada or the United States: a suspiciously even 5,280 feet, or 1 mile. The total drop is about a thousand feet greater than Jackson Hole, which promotes itself as the tallest slope in the

United States (4,139 feet). At least twenty-one North American resorts have a vertical drop of at least 3,000 feet. Only one, Killington, is in the East (3,160 feet). In comparison, many smaller resorts a few hours' drive from Eastern cities do well enough with a drop of 1,000 feet or less.

Vertical-drop statistics usually apply to resorts rather than individual runs. That can be misleading. The resort measurements represent the difference in elevation between the highest point on the resort's highest ski run and the lowest point on the lowest run. You wouldn't in every case ski down the full drop at once. As resorts tend to merge or expand onto neighboring mountains, the statistic becomes even less meaningful. Statistics on individual runs are more to the point.

Despite Whistler/Blackcomb's preeminence, it gilds the lily with claims of a "9,000-plus vertical." This means if you take the vertical on Whistler Mountain and add it to Blackcomb's, the sum is over 9,000 feet. This is absurd. There are plenty of resorts and resort complexes with half a dozen skiable mountains. Totaling their verticals would produce equally impressive and meaningless numbers.

It's not just the vertical distance that makes a run difficult. It's how quickly you descend it—which is mainly a matter of how steep the run is. Statistics on grade of runs are even more approximate and misleading than vertical drops. It is difficult to measure the inclination of a mountain, even at one point. The slope varies, so it can be deceptive to single out one value. Even the "average slope" is ambiguous.

None of this prevents skiers from having opinions about which mountains are steeper than others and attempting to justify those opinions with numbers. The *Guinness Book of*

*World Records,* for instance, states that the steepest ski descent was that of Sylvain Saudan, who skied the northeast slope of Mont Blanc on "gradients in excess of 60 degrees." Other notable descents are comparable. Jean Marc Boivin skied down the east face of the Matterhorn, which is alleged to have a slope of 65 degrees. These feats were not done on regular ski runs but on wild mountains.

In 1980, *Ski* magazine published a list of "the steepest and longest runs in the U.S." This they defined as the steepest lift-served runs of at least 4,000 feet in length. The steepest such run was Sun Valley's Christmas Bowl.

| Run | | Average Slope (degrees) | Vertical Drop (feet) |
|---|---|---|---|
| Christmas Bowl | Sun Valley, Idaho | 35.9 | 2,240 |
| Gros Ventre | Jackson Hole, Wyo. | 30.0 | 2,000 |
| Al's Run | Taos, N.M. | 26.7 | 1,800 |
| U.N. Trail | Jay Peak, Vt. | 26.7 | 1,800 |
| International | Alpental, Wash. | 25.9 | 2,400 |
| Madonna | Smuggler's Notch, Vt. | 25.8 | 2,300 |
| Gunbarrel | Heavenly Valley, Calif. | 25.2 | 1,700 |
| Skyward | Whiteface, N.Y. | 24.0 | 1,870 |
| Grizzly | Montana Snowbowl, Mont. | 23.6 | 2,000 |
| North Hoback | Jackson Hole, Wyo. | 23.6 | 2,000 |

This list is okay as far as it goes. The catch is the requirement that the runs be 4,000 feet long (measured diagonally, as you would actually ski). A run is defined more by its worst parts than by some hypothetical average. One good suicide plunge makes a run daunting even if the rest of it is easy. Fear isn't logical.

The list includes longish runs that are *consistently* steep over their length. Christmas Bowl's average slope of 35.9 degrees doesn't sound all that steep, and it's not. What's exceptional is that this is the *average* slope over nearly a mile of skiing (4,875 feet, to be exact). Parts of the run are steeper than 35.9 degrees, and parts are less steep.

That still doesn't mean that Christmas Bowl is extraordinarily steep at any one point. It doesn't mean that Christmas Bowl is tougher than other slopes, which are considerably steeper at their worst.

If you took the steepest runs (or portions of runs) at least 1,000 feet long, you would probably get a different list. If you took the steepest runs 500 feet long, you'd have still another list. The shorter the minimum distance, the greater the slopes would be. There is no long run that is on a 45-degree diagonal, but there are plenty of short runs and parts of runs that are. There are even shorter runs that are sheerer yet. A segment of run does not have to be long to be scary. There would appear to be some optimum scale for maximum pumping of adrenaline: possibly a few tens or hundreds of feet?

It might seem that the steepest possible inclination for a ski slope is 90 degrees, a vertical cliff. Actually, the slope can be greater, creating a concave overhang. You can have a 100-degree "slope," 110 degrees, 120 degrees . . .

There *are* overhanging mountains, and some of them are skied. One such overhang is at the top of Corbet's Couloir at Jackson Hole, and another is the Palisades at Squaw Valley, Calif.

The exact degree of overhang is somewhat beside the point. You don't ski the underside of an overhang. You jump off the top of the cliff and fall almost vertically onto a slope below. The meaningful point of comparison is the vertical height of overhang. It is the minimum distance you must *fall* in skiing off the overhang. If you went to the very edge of the precipice and dropped a plumb line to the slope below, the length of the line would be the height of overhang.

In both of the runs mentioned, the overhang is partly created by drifting tongues of ice and snow. It therefore varies with season and snowfall. Corbet's Couloir has the greater overhang height and may fairly be judged the toughest, scariest ski run in North America. A couloir is a natural chute of snow or ice packed into the trench between two ridges. Corbet's Couloir proper is a short (900 feet vertical drop) ultra-steep run averaging a 45-degree diagonal. Depending on how the snow is packed, the pitch may be as much as 50 degrees.

We're interested in the overhanging part. To ski Corbet's Couloir, you have to jump off the overhang onto the highly pitched slope below. The height of overhang is about 15 feet. Since you arc out in a parabola, the actual free fall is more like 25 feet. If you can't land like a cat, you are liable to slide all the way to the bottom.

Those who have skied it successfully have a technique. The instructors recommend that you relax but check the reflex to sit back. Otherwise, you slam down into the snow and slide all the way down. (Since it is underneath the tram, everyone sees you.) Even aside from the leap, Corbet's Couloir is a difficult short run. It is narrow, requiring a dogleg in the middle, and girt with rocks. Although it is all but anticlimactic, there are 3,000 more feet of mountain below Corbet's Couloir.

# THE BEST BASEBALL PLAYER OF ALL TIME

# WHO IS THE BEST

baseball player of all time? Like most nagging questions that never really get answered, this one is childishly simple and direct. The adult in us insists that baseball is a complex game requiring a number of distinct, incommensurable skills. Yeah, but who's the best player?

Babe Ruth is the best player of the twentieth century, according to Bill James's thoughtful number crunching in the *Historical Baseball Abstract*. Gene Karst and Martin J. Jones in their *Who's Who in Professional Baseball* (1973) agree that Ruth is "undoubtedly the greatest of all players when versatility is considered." "What can anyone say about Babe Ruth that has not already been said, except to insist that he, the Babe, not anyone else, was the greatest baseball player who ever lived?" rhetorically asks Joseph L. Reichler in *The World Series: 76th Anniversary Edition* (1979).

But Willie Mays is really the best player of this century, insists sportswriter Maury Allen in his 1981 book, *Baseball's 100*. Allen thinks Ruth is good but kind of overrated.

The best player is Mickey Mantle, specifically his 1957 season, according to Thomas Cover of Stanford University. Cover based that conclusion on his pet statistic, the offensive earned-run average.

That Napoleon Lajoie is the best player who ever lived is the odd thesis of Charles F. Faber and his 1985 book, *Baseball Ratings.* Faber assigns players points, and Lajoie rakes in 3,196 of them. Babe Ruth is a distant second with 2,869 points. (Lajoie played second base for Philadelphia and Cleveland from 1896 to 1916, and most people who saw him are dead.)

Lawrence Ritter and Donald Honig's *The 100 Greatest Baseball Players of All Time* (1986) cops out by listing players in what they insist is "more or less random sequence." It's not alphabetical and not chronological. Their 100 begins with Pete Rose and ends with Dizzy Dean.

The closest thing to an official opinion is the voting for Most Valuable Player awards. The MVP voters are presumably knowledgeable people (members of the Baseball Writers' Association), selecting each season's best players, while memory is fresh. Jimmy Foxx, Joe DiMaggio, Stan Musial, Yogi Berra, Roy Campanella, Mickey Mantle, and Mike Schmidt have won three MVP awards each, and three is the most anyone has ever won. If you add up the total MVP votes in all years—Bill James does this in the *Historical Baseball Abstract*—the player who received the most votes over his career is Stan Musial. That would appear to say that Stan Musial is the best player over his career, in the era the award has existed.

Even this doesn't exhaust the diversity of opinion. Ty Cobb, Walter Johnson, Cy Young, and Buck Ewing have each been seriously championed by reasonable people as the best player of all time.

The attempts to single out an all-time best player can be divided into left-brain and right-brain approaches. Some veteran sportswriters have set out to decide which player, in their opinion and on the basis of their recollections, was best. The trouble is, baseball writers and fans are an awfully sentimental lot. You have to wonder if they are capable of comparing today's players with the memories of their youth without a certain nostalgic bias. Worse, this approach demands an encyclopedic knowledge of the game that no one now has. Anyone who remembers seeing Babe Ruth is getting up there. No one coherently remembers the hotshot 1906–8 Chicago Cubs.

It would be easy to sigh and dismiss the best-player question if we had to rely on muddled recollections of old-timers. We don't. What makes the question of best player so tantalizing is that we do have a statistical record of the game's history. The statistics *should* reveal the best player.

Of course, it's not that simple. As even the most casual baseball fans know, statistics are treacherous. In 1930, *everyone* in the St. Louis Cardinals' starting lineup batted over .300. Today a team counts itself lucky to have even *one* .300 hitter. Aside from a few curmudgeonly old-timers, no one thinks that today's best batters are less competent than the .400 hitters of old. The game's dynamics have changed somehow.

Rules, strategies, training methods, and the stadiums have changed; night games have been introduced. Most important, the players themselves have changed. There is little doubt that, with the money involved, there is a greater, more consistent level of professionalism than there was around the turn of the century. Unfortunately, we *have* to compare records from throughout the history of baseball to determine the all-time best player. So the statistical record has to be put in context.

People are more sensible about financial statistics than baseball statistics. If it was a question of best-paid player, we wouldn't dote on unqualified trivia like so-and-so had a zilliondollar contract. We would insist that it's *salary* rather than the gross amount of money that counts—how much a player earned per year, per game, or per some unit of time. We would insist that any value be compared with what other players were making at the time. We can't evaluate the fact that Babe Ruth made $80,000 a season in isolation; what were the other players, or the average guys in the stands, making? Athletic statistics must be qualified in much the same way.

There are two distinct ways of looking at "best player of all time." Is it the best player at the peak of his form, or is it the player who contributed the most over his entire career?

Say some guy comes out of the minors, plays the best season anyone has ever seen, and then drops dead. That would probably make him a legend. Honig and Ritter call this the "Smokey Joe Wood Syndrome." Wood did great in 1912, then injured his arm in the spring of 1913 and never recovered. They claim he was good enough in that one season to qualify as one of the 100 best players of all time.

More often a player has a choice in the matter. He may decide to quit while he's ahead or to continue playing long past his peak. Some statistics, like runs scored, keep piling up, if at a trickle, in a player's waning years. A player with the knack of maintaining a level of acceptable performance year in and year out could attain enormous cumulative statistics. On the other hand, years of post-peak performance pull down career averages like batting average and ERA.

James's *Historical Baseball Almanac* addresses both issues

separately. (James considers Babe Ruth the best whether you go by his peak season or consider his whole career.) Many other sources apparently muddle the two issues. Longevity is probably more important to team management and to a player's potential for product endorsements, but it's not primarily what people think of when talking about a best player. A mediocre player cannot become any better through seniority. The best player is the player who played the best—even if for a single summer.

Longevity shouldn't count for anything, nor should it penalize (assuming that the player did indeed spend his peak years playing major-league ball). For convenience' sake, let's define the peak to be a season. If you tried to decide who had the best month, or the best day, you'd be looking at luck, not skill.

Some divvy the best-player question up by position. They name someone as best first baseman, someone else as best shortstop, and so on. There's nothing wrong with this. It does not replace the central question of who was the best player of all. The fact remains that some one player playing one particular position was the most valuable to his team. If, say, left field is a less crucial position than pitcher, then so be it. It's less likely that the best player was a left fielder.

Baseball is a team sport. The trick is deconstructing each player's contribution to the runs scored, and ultimately to games won. Fortunately, there is a consensus about how to start. Baseball and most popular team sports have many features in common. Teams score points (runs in baseball) until a fixed number of time units or play units (outs in baseball) have been exhausted. The team with the higher number of points wins. The average number of points scored is high enough so that ties are rare.

You want to be able to evaluate players by plugging the box-score statistics into a formula (embodied in a computer program usually) and having a number pop out that tells how good he was. That's what statistics nuts hope for, anyway. The hard part is designing the formula.

The proper approach, used by all progressive statistical systems, is to estimate what a player produces and divide it by what he consumes. The result (something like runs/outs) allows you to project what a team composed of exact duplicates of the player would score.

This statistical fiction can be compared with the average and thereby evaluated. You can figure what percentage of games an all-Babe Ruth clone team would have won playing against the other teams in the league. If a team of Babe Ruth clones would have racked up a higher win percentage than a team of Willie Mays clones, then Babe Ruth was the better player.

Baseball is two interleaved games: hitting and fielding. Most of the familiar player statistics measure hitting and base running—offense. That's mainly because it's clear who's scoring hits and runs. *Preventing* the opposing team from scoring is a team effort.

It does not necessarily follow that a good hitter is a good fielder. Nonetheless, there is justification for the emphasis on offense. The defensive skills of any one player are less critical than his offensive skills. When a player is at bat, it's him against the aggregate of the opposing team. If the batter is lousy, his team isn't going to score. When an individual fielder is weak, his teammates can to some extent cover for him. A first-rate hitter who's a weak fielder may be acceptable; a bad hitter who's a good fielder is a liability.

You can justify this numerically. As will be shown, the difference in runs created between a Babe Ruth and an average hitter can be as many as 200 runs a season. The difference in runs allowed between the best defensive team and the worst is usually a bit over 200 runs. The combined skills of the best defensive team in a league (plus park effects!) suffice to nullify the efforts of a single extraordinary hitter.

For this reason, one must discount most arguments to the effect that "so-and-so was a great hitter but lousy at defense, and therefore not as good as so-and-so." It's possible for defensive weakness to undermine hitting strengths, of course, but such imbalances tend to be exaggerated—especially among first-class hitters. Had Babe Ruth taken a nap in right field, he could hardly have sabotaged the Yankees' defense to the tune of 200 runs a season. And rarely are players that one-dimensional. A first-class hitter may not be *as* good at defense. His fielding suffers by comparison.

So let's start by looking at offensive statistics, with the proviso that we consider the defensive record once the field has been narrowed.

Dozens of exotic statistical formulas have been devised for rating players. You get the impression that the average statistician starts with a pretty strong opinion about who's the best player and expects to see that opinion confirmed. If not, he fine-tunes the formula. It's a vicious circle. The only way a formula gains credibility is by confirming the conventional wisdom, yet a statistical method is of no value unless it tells us something we don't already know. It has to challenge the conventional wisdom some of the time.

Most formulas "work," in the sense that if you figure the value for all players and take the top ten by that formula, you don't have any oddball entries on the list. The challenge is knowing which statistics are the most relevant ones.

Baseball is not a matter of hitting home runs, not really, and it's not a matter of getting a high batting average either. The best player is the one who was responsible for his team winning the most games. The way you win ball games is by scoring more runs than the other team.

That leads us to two box-score statistics, runs and runs batted in. Neither is the index of the player's ability that you might hope for. With the notable exception of a home run, the run that a player scores is a collaboration between that player and those who batted after him. When a player hits a home run, he is contributing to the runs scored by players already on base. RBIs are a collaboration with the previous batters.

You can't shrug this off. Sophisticated lineup strategies often distort run and RBI statistics out of recognition. That Babe Ruth scored a record 171 runs in the 1921 season is tough to square with the fact that the season RBI record belongs to a relative nonentity, Lewis "Hack" Wilson (190 in 1930). Few think Wilson was all that great.

We want some fair way of going beyond the box scores, of

deciding who's really responsible for each run. (Typically the credit will have to be split among several players.) In recent years, statistically minded fans have devised computer models that apportion credit for runs *precisely*. These models require painstakingly complete record keeping. You have to know who (if anyone) was on each base before and after every at bat in the game. Such systems are eminently fair. They are beside the point here, however. No one kept such detailed records for old games.

It is too late now to decide we need information that wasn't recorded. The conventional statistics are incomplete enough. We can't trace baseball back to its primordial ooze (mid-1800s). There just aren't systematic statistics. It's doubtful, though, that anyone who played back then was as good or professional as later players. More disappointing is the lack of statistics on the Negro leagues. Satchel Paige is often cited as having been among the best players of all time. There isn't enough of a statistical record to test this conclusion.

We need an approximate runs-created formula that works from the usual box-score statistics of the major leagues. Of several such formulas, by far the best-known is that used by Bill James in his *Historical Baseball Abstract*.

James played around with the statistics and found a formula connecting a team's total hits, walks, stolen bases, total bases, at bats, and so forth with its total runs. There is no ironclad relationship between runs and the other statistics, but there is a strong correlation. A team that gets a lot of hits and walks usually gets a lot of runs. James actually uses at least fourteen variants of the formula. They are all close to this basic version:

$$\text{Runs Created} =$$
$$[(\text{Hits} + \text{Walks}) \times (\text{Total Bases})] / (\text{At Bats} + \text{Walks})$$

Other versions of the formula introduce corrections and refinements for different historical periods. The essential point is that this formula does a pretty good job of predicting a team's (already known) number of runs from its other statistics.

There would be no point in that except that the statistics the formula uses are the same statistics that are tabulated for each player. Therefore, you can plug in a player's individual statistics and the formula will crank out an estimate of how many runs that player was responsible for.

You might figure, as a first approximation, that the player responsible for the most runs in a season is the best player—at least, the best offensive player. By James's calculations, that would be Babe Ruth. Ruth created 238 runs in 1921, which is more than anyone else in any one season. Ruth's career total, 2,843 runs, is also the highest.

Runs alone can be misleading. You don't talk of hits; you talk of a batting average. For the same reason, runs created is not as pertinent as a ratio. You might use runs per at bat. Much more reasonable is runs per out.

The out is the time unit of baseball. Football and basketball run by the clock; baseball ticks by its own Silly Putty time units, outs and innings. If no one scored any outs, an inning would last forever and have a score of infinity. Outs, not minutes or at bats, are the nonrenewable resource that puts urgency into the game.

The value of a player to a team is in the runs he produces from the outs he is allotted. A player who never, ever was called out would be pure gravy. His runs would be "free." The more runs a player produces per out, the more valuable he is. Divide each player's runs or bases by the total of that player's outs (outs at bat, outs while attempting to steal bases, and outs from sacrifice bunts and flies and ground-ball double plays). An advantage of using runs created per out is that it equitably treats players who, because of batting order or days lost to injuries, were at bat fewer times than others.

James prefers to use runs per game. A typical game of 9 innings has 27 outs for each team. Statistics show that the actual number of outs per team is very close to 27, extra-inning games tending to cancel out the effect of rain calls and home teams that don't bat in the ninth inning. You can multiply runs per out by 27 to get runs per game. (Actually, we must use 26 outs for players of Ruth's era because the incomplete statistics kept then account for only about 26 outs, on the average, per game.) You can likewise multiply runs per game by the number of games in any season to get a player's runs per season.

Runs per game does not reflect how many runs the team did score in any game. It is rather what the team *would have* scored in an average game if everyone batted exactly like the player in question. It is how many runs a team of clones of that player would be expected to score in an average game.

This still doesn't permit direct historic comparisons. Runs were cheaper back in Ruth's day: Everyone scored more runs. Directly comparing runs created across chasms of baseball history is as fallacious as comparing batting averages. Things have changed. We need to compare a player's runs per game with what teams were scoring on the average.

There are several ways of doing this. In Pete Palmer and

John Thorn's *The Hidden Game of Baseball* (1984), they subtract the league's average runs from each player's runs created. The result is negative for a poor player, zero for a player completely average in the league, and positive for a good player. The value tells, or purports to tell, exactly how many runs the team is ahead for having that player rather than an average player. The best player is the one with the highest (positive) rating.

An even more concrete way of expressing things is to calculate how many *wins* a player was responsible for. This is what James does in his *Historical Baseball Abstract*. If a team with nine players wins 90 games and if all the players contribute equally, then each player was responsible for 10 victories. If the players *don't* contribute equally, maybe you can find grounds for claiming that the pitcher was responsible for 14 wins, while the right fielder created only 8, and so on. James uses the individual runs created to mete out credit for a team's wins and losses. To do this, he uses his "Pythagorean approach to winning percentage."

Now take a deep breath. James's claim is that the square of a team's runs scored divided by the square of its runs allowed equals (approximately) the number of wins divided by losses. Rearranging this to get a win percentage:

$$\text{Win Percentage} = (\text{Runs Scored})^2 / [(\text{Runs Scored})^2 + (\text{Runs Allowed})^2]$$

James provides not a shred of justification for it, other than the fact that *it actually does work*. For instance, take the Toronto Blue Jays in the 1984 season. They scored 750 runs and allowed 696. Multiply 750 by itself and you get 562,500. Divide that by 696 squared (484,416) and the result is 1.161. That means that the Blue Jays should have won 1.161 games for every one they lost. Or to put it as the conventional percentage of wins divided by wins plus losses, it would be 1.161 / (1 + 1.161) or .537. Since the Blue Jays played 162 games, you would expect 87 wins and 75 losses.

In fact, the Blue Jays won 89 games and lost 73. (The win percentage was .549.) The differences between the actual and predicted wins are almost always small, rarely exceeding four games in a season. The discrepancies are about evenly split between positives and negatives.

This allows us to project an "offensive winning percentage" for individual players. Take a player and clone a whole team's worth of him. Everyone on this team hits exactly the same way. Let this team play a regular season (against the same opponents and in the same stadiums as did the player in question). We already have the player's runs created per game. For runs allowed, use the actual runs scored of the player's team's opponents. The offensive winning percentage is the proportion of games the clone team would win, based on the Pythagorean formula.

One nice thing about this system is that it factors out park effects. It is a well-known fact that some parks favor hitters and others fielders. Wrigley Field is good for hitters; Dodger Stadium favors fielders. You can't say all things come out in the wash because the Cubs play half their games in Wrigley Field, and the Dodgers half theirs in Dodger Stadium.

Park effects don't make any great difference in how many

games a team wins. Each team takes its turn playing the advantaged and disadvantaged sides. The park effect does inflate some statistics, though. The Cubs have more hits at home than away. Since half their games are at home, we must conclude that the Cubs have more hits in a season than they would if they were playing in a hypothetical average park. It's not unfair, because the Cubs' opponents also have more hits when playing in Wrigley Field, but it does skew the statistics.

James's system excises park effects by comparing a player's runs created with those of his team's collective opponents. In his system, you add up the runs created by the team's opponents in every game they played against the team. The opponents always played in the same stadium as the team did.

You don't have to buy this. You may insist that a team is a team and it makes no more sense to say that so many runs were due to one player than to say how much of an ovation is due to left hands. But if you choose to talk about relative contributions of players to a team, and if you believe that contributions are reflected in statistics, then James's formulas make a lot of sense.

An offensive win percentage of .500 is exactly average. A value of .800 is pretty spectacular. By James's accounting, the player with the best offensive win percentage *over his entire career* is Ted Williams, with .858. A team of Ted Williams clones playing the teams Williams actually played would probably win about 86 percent of their games. To further the statistical conceit, you can say that Williams was responsible for winning 168 games and losing 28 over his career.

Babe Ruth is second in career win percentage with .851. (The exact values have varied as James has tweaked his formulas, and Ruth has occasionally come out narrowly ahead. It now seems likely that Williams's lead is established.)

We're mainly interested in peak seasons. In 1920, his best year, Ruth achieved a win percentage of .934. In effect, he was responsible for 11 of the Yankees' wins that year and only 1 of the losses. That's very, very good. But it's not the best win percentage ever.

Some players would rate anomalously high win percentages for a "season" because they played in only a few games. They happened to do well and not be put out much. Paul Waner did that in the 1945 season, when he played in exactly one game and got one walk. You could calculate a high value for this "season," but it's pointless. The same goes for Larry Gardner in 1908 (played in two games), Max Carey in 1910 (two games), Ray Schalk in 1928 (two games), and Tony Oliva in 1962 (nine games).

In 1925, his first year in the majors, Jimmy Foxx played in 10 games. He was at bat 9 times, got 6 hits and 2 runs. James calculates that Foxx created 4 runs for the team (Philadelphia) and that his corresponding win percentage would be .983. Foxx went on to be an outstanding first baseman in the 1920s and 1930s, but he never achieved a win percentage higher than .865 when playing full seasons. Evidently the 1925 figure was a fluke, too.

When we talk about a player's best season, we mean the best one in which he played full-time or nearly so. Shall we say at least 100 games? Then the player with the highest percentage for a full season is Mickey Mantle. In 1957 his offensive win percentage was .935.

|  | Season | Offensive Win Percentage |
|---|---|---|
| Mickey Mantle | 1957 | 0.935 |
| Babe Ruth | 1920 | 0.934 |
| Ted Williams | 1957 | 0.932 |
| Ted Williams | 1941 | 0.931 |
| Babe Ruth | 1923 | 0.928 |
| Ted Williams | 1946 | 0.914 |
| Babe Ruth | 1921 | 0.913 |
| Babe Ruth | 1924 | 0.911 |
| Ted Williams | 1942 | 0.911 |
| Ted Williams | 1947 | 0.909 |
| Ted Williams | 1954 | 0.908 |
| Babe Ruth | 1926 | 0.904 |
| Arky Vaughan | 1935 | 0.902 |
| Rogers Hornsby | 1924 | 0.900 |

Notice how iffy the ranking is! Ruth (1920 season) comes in second to Mantle by a difference so trifling (.001) that you can't feel very good about judging Mantle the better player on that alone. The difference is too minuscule to account for even a single additional victory. Both Ruth in 1920 and Mantle in 1957 effectively won 11 games and lost 1 for their teams.

Ted Williams's 1957 season comes in third by another paper-thin margin. To confuse things further, Williams played a number of incomplete seasons in which his win percentage would be higher than Mantle's. Williams's peak "year" was 1952, when he was in Korea with the Marines and played in only six games. His fragmentary statistics qualify him for a theoretical win percentage of .963. He was virtually as good in 1953 (.962), when he played in 37 games. Another season that barely misses the above list is 1955, when a slip in the shower and pneumonia restricted him to 98 games. He rated .911 that year.

It's one thing to ignore the incomplete seasons of guys like Waner and Foxx. Williams, however, has been seriously championed as the best player of all time. In 1952 and 1953 he played in 43 games, in which his average win percentage was about .962. That's not so few games that you can easily dismiss it, especially since the percentage is considerably larger than Mantle's 1957 record.

In evaluating such small differences, it is important to know how trustworthy the statistics are. James's runs-created formulas are not precise. He estimates that they have an average error of about 20 runs in predicting a team's actual runs for the season from the raw statistics. That amounts to a 3 percent average error out of 670 runs or so. This is squared to get the win percentage, which multiplies the error to about 6 percent. (The runs-created estimate is in the range of 0.97 to 1.03 times the actual value; the square of this will be 0.94 to 1.06 times the square of the actual value.)

That kind of error would swamp the fine distinctions above. A 6 percent margin of error means that Mantle's .935 record could actually be as low as .879 or as high as .991. Any one of the players on the list could have the highest "real" win percentage. So could some not on the list. That's not to say that Mantle's lead is meaningless. Mantle is still most likely, on the basis of the statistics, to be the best player. We just can't be very dogmatic about it.

Things aren't necessarily as ambiguous as that. Arguably, the James formula is a measure of a player's ability in its own right. That it correlates with the runs scored in actual play is lagniappe. The "error" is irrelevant. Even if you take that position, there are concerns about statistical significance. Could a single lucky hit or bad call sometime in the season have taken away Mantle's lead?

It could. Consider what just *one* fortuitous hit more or less would do to the rankings. In 1957 Mantle had 173 hits, 146 walks, 315 total bases, and 474 at bats. The simplest version of the runs-created formula goes $(173 + 146) \times 315 / (474 + 146)$. That means Mantle created 162 runs. Had Mantle got an extra hit it would have made a difference of about three-tenths of 1 percent (162.58 with 174 hits vs. 162.07 for 173 hits). The James formula divides this by outs and then squares it. Squaring a small margin of error doubles it, so the difference in the win percentage due to a lucky hit becomes six-tenths of a percent.

This is enough to upset the Mantle/Ruth/Williams pecking order. We're saying that if Mantle had muffed a single hit, his win percentage of .935 would drop to .929. An extra hit would have raised Ruth's 1920 percentage to .940; one less would have lowered it to .928. Williams's 1957 record is bracketed by .938 and .926.

Baseball is not always fair. A player is liable to have a few lucky hits in a season and to be robbed of a few. Though Mantle has the highest offensive win percentage, it is grasping at straws to cite him over Ruth and Williams as the best offensive player.

Some take the solipsistic position that only the statistics matter. The seasons of yesteryear are gone. Only the statistics remain, and only the statistics matter. A lead, however narrow, is a lead. But most people are interested in the players as defined by the statistics and not the statistics per se. Sometimes the statistics allow a conclusion about who's better, and sometimes they don't. Anyone insisting that Mantle is the best player on the basis of his hitting statistics is placing more confidence in the statistics than they deserve. It is like concluding from a census report that the number of inhabitants of Chicago is an even number.

Are there any other reasons to favor Mantle, Ruth, or Williams? Well, there's a long list of baseball-card distinctions we haven't mentioned. Ruth hit more home runs than Mantle (54 vs. 34 in 1920 and 1957). He had a higher batting average (.376 vs. .365). But remember, this has already been figured in. Home runs and hits are only means toward the end of scoring more runs than the other team. It has already been established that Ruth and Mantle were responsible for nearly the same number of runs per out, normalized by the league average.

There is still defense to consider. Defense statistics are equivocal. At bat, everyone has an equal chance to score runs. Not all defensive positions are equally important. You would be hard put to cite a game in which a really, really good catcher was responsible for his team winning. That doesn't mean the catcher is deadwood; it's just hard to be sure how important he is.

Range factor, the single most quoted fielding statistic, illustrates the ambiguity. (The range factor is the number of balls that player fielded that resulted in putting a runner out, per an average game's worth of batted balls.) One feels safer saying that a high range factor is good than that a low range factor is damning. If no one hits the ball his way, a player is going to have a low range factor no matter how good he is. More than that, if a player is known to be a hotshot fielder, batters are going to do their best to *avoid* hitting balls his way.

Both Mantle and Ruth had quite respectable range factors. Mantle had ten seasons with a range factor over 2.00; Ruth had eleven. Neither player's peak range factor coincided with their peak offensive season. Mantle's best range factor was 2.74, in 1953. Ruth's best was 2.69, in 1923.

We'll look at the peak hitting seasons rather than the peak seasons for range factor because the all-round "best" season is determined almost entirely by runs created. Mantle in 1957 had a higher range factor than Ruth in 1920, who had a higher factor than Williams in 1957. Ruth's statistics must be compared cautiously with the other two players'. So many things changed in the intervening years. However, Mantle's and Williams's peak hitting seasons coincided, and they played in the same league.

All things considered, there can be little doubt that Mantle was more important to the 1957 Yankees' defense than Ruth was to the 1920 Yankees' or Williams was to the 1957 Red Sox':

|                  | Range Factor | Putouts | Assists | Fielding % |
|------------------|:------------:|:-------:|:-------:|:----------:|
| Mantle (1957)    | 2.37         | 324     | 6       | 0.979      |
| Ruth (1920)      | 2.01         | 259     | 21      | 0.936      |
| Williams (1957)  | 1.74         | 215     | 2       | 0.995      |

The range factor can be thought of as the number of outs for the opposing team created by the player. It is a better measure than actual putouts because it is adjusted for an average game's worth of batted balls. Every out created deprived the opposing team of 1/27 of its opportunity to score runs. Figuring that an average team in an average game scores about 4 runs, we can guesstimate that one out is the equivalent of 0.15 run.

Multiply the range factor by 0.15 and you have an estimate of how many runs the player's fielding cost the opposing team. In an average game, Mantle's fielding cost the opposing team 2.37 times 0.15, or 0.36 run. That means Mantle increased the 1957 Yankees' margin of victory (or decreased its margin of loss) by 0.36 run a game. Ruth's fielding cost the opposing team only 0.30 run (and runs were cheaper back then), and Williams prevented 0.26 run a game.

It is risky to project these figures onto a whole field of player clones. But however you figure it, the defensive statistics increase Mantle's slight lead over Ruth. They provide little or no ground for saying Ruth was really the better player.

There is another point to consider—possibly the most controversial of all. Americans are getting bigger.

Lincoln was the Illinois Giant in his time; today he'd be on the short side. In most track and field events, athletes have gotten steadily faster and stronger over the past half century. There is better nutrition and childhood care; people grow taller and healthier; longer legs mean faster runners. Training methods and sports medicine have improved, too.

Call this the Wonder Bread effect. It must apply to baseball, too. Baseball is, after all, a game of running and throwing. The difference is that baseball players compete not against a clock or measuring rod but against other players. These players, on the average, run faster and throw harder, too. Thus in baseball, unlike track and field, the ever-increasing level of athletic skill is not chronicled in a chain of broken records.

Besides the Wonder Bread effect, there's a population factor. Today's top athletes are drawn from a population that is much greater than that of the 1920s. The greater the population base, the tougher the competition for the few major-league positions. You would expect that the fastest runner or the most accurate thrower out of 242 million people would be better than the best in 123 million.

These long-term changes have been used to bolster arguments for the superiority of more recent players to older ones. Almost four decades separate Ruth's peak from Mantle's. If the players in Ruth's time were a little smaller, slower, and less powerful than those in Mantle's time, it would be further reason to consider Mantle's record superior to Ruth's. It is important to realize that any such effect would be above and beyond what is shown in the usual statistics. All regular statistics are relative. The batting average depends not just on the skill of the player but also on the aggregate skill of the opposing team's pitchers and whether the player can run faster than the opposition. Nor are the clever constructs of statisticians exempt. Runs created and offensive win percentages are relative, too.

The gist of the debate is this: Suppose you had a time machine and went back to the 1920s. You scoop up Babe Ruth at his peak and bring him back to the present to play on a team today. *Would he be as good?*

One guesses—it's only a guess, one that many have ventured —that today's Wonder Bread-fed players would give Ruth a harder time. His batting average would be decent, but in line with today's players' averages. It is not even clear how outstanding a player he would be. Our knowledge of Ruth is based on how good he was playing against the players of his time.

That raises a philosophical point about "best player." Do we mean the player who was most outstanding in his milieu? Or do we mean the objectively best player, the one who would win some sort of time-machine round-robin tournament against all the other greats of baseball history?

The latter is the more appealing conception. Suppose for the sake of argument that the best ball player in Japan ("the Babe Ruth of Japan") tries out for an American team. It turns out that he is only a mediocre player when competing with the Americans. Is he a better or a worse player than the Americans? In a sense he's better because he's the national hero. In another sense he's worse because he comes off second best in actual competition. Most people would probably say he was not as good. Therefore it is relevant to consider how the level of competition may have changed.

Any glib discussion of changing standards must start by mentioning that Ruth was *taller* than Mantle. He stood 6 feet 2 inches, which was big for his time. His weight yo-yoed up and down, from 185 to 270 pounds over his career. Mantle was only 6 feet even, and not considered especially tall. He weighed about 201 pounds.

But the *player's* height is not the issue. Any advantage (or disadvantage) accruing from it has already been expressed in the statistics. The height of the player's *opponents* is another thing. If Ruth played against players who were smaller and less strong or fast in an absolute sense, then it would be proper to adjust our opinion of his skills.

The records chronicle a modest long-term increase in the size of professional baseball players. In the 1920 World Series, the average height was 5 feet 11¼ inches. In the 1957 Series, the average was 6 feet ½ inch. (At that, several proverbially diminutive Yankees dragged down the 1957 average: Yogi Berra, Enos Slaughter, and Bobby Shantz.) This implies that the average height of major-league ballplayers has been increasing at the rate of about an inch every thirty years.

If these figures are representative, the average player Ruth played against in 1920 was about 1.25 inches shorter and must have weighed something like 5 pounds less than the average player Mantle confronted in 1957. That would mean an average 1957 player's leg would be about three-quarters of an inch

| 1920 World Series | Avg. Height | 1957 World Series | Avg. Height |
| --- | --- | --- | --- |
| Cleveland | 70.91 | Milwaukee | 73.21 |
| Brooklyn | 71.75 | New York | 71.85 |
| Both teams | 71.26 | Both teams | 72.50 |

longer and take in proportionately more real estate with each stride.

Hard evidence that a modest increase in height translates into stronger ball-playing skills is sparse. Three objective measures on which records have been kept are baserunning speed, pitch speed, and length of hit.

According to the *Guinness Book of World Records,* in 1921 a minor-leaguer named Maurice Archdeacon set a record by circling the bases in 13.4 seconds. This was not in a game. Archdeacon was in the minors, so you have to assume that the players in the majors weren't much more sluggish. Archdeacon's record was narrowly bettered in 1932, when Ernest Evar Swanson traversed the diamond in 13.3 seconds. The latter record still stands.

The *Guinness Book of World Records'* fastest pitch is that of Nolan Ryan. In 1974 he threw a ball that was clocked at 100.9 miles per hour.

Finally, the Guinness folks credit Mickey Mantle with having hit the longest home run. The longest officially measured home run of Mantle's was 565 feet. However, the famous homer of

September 10, 1960, which landed in a Detroit lumberyard, was measured trigonometrically as 643 feet in 1985.

Of these three records, one goes back to Ruth's time and two are from Mantle's time or later. One record *is* Mantle's. The most reasonable conclusion is that Mantle's 1957 teammates and opponents were slightly stronger and swifter, in absolute terms, than the players in Ruth's peak season.

Going by career achievement, there can be no doubt that Babe Ruth was the best player of all time. He played longer than Mantle or Williams. He played at near-peak level a lot longer than Mantle did.

The distinct question of who was the best at his peak is primarily what we have set out to answer. There the evidence favors Mantle's 1957 season. He is barely ahead of Ruth and Williams by the most reasonable measures of hitting power. Defensive statistics rate Mantle over Ruth, and the historic increase in the size and skills of athletes tends to favor Mantle over Ruth as well.

# THE BEST
# FOOTBALL
# PLAYER
# OF ALL TIME

# JIM THORPE'S

contemporaries hailed him as the best football player ever. It was not something people debated; if you understood the game, you knew Thorpe was best. Besides, he was a pro baseball player, an Olympic pentathlon and decathlon star, and possibly the best athlete ever, too. Yet it is impossible to get much idea of why Thorpe was so good from statistics. Few football statistics were kept in Thorpe's time. The figures we can reconstruct from newspaper accounts make it sound like he was playing on Mars. No one passed, scores were low, yet Thorpe's Canton Bulldogs creamed the opposition. In Thorpe's first four years, the 'Dogs lost only twice. Thorpe was doing something right, and clearly the game was a lot different back then.

The game of football has changed so fundamentally that inter-era comparisons are the most problematic of the major team sports. There is a cynicism about the whole question of "best" football player, a feeling that the sport has redefined itself to the point where the past (pre-1960, anyway) just doesn't count.

Systematic football statistics date from 1935. Of players in the statistical era, Sammy Baugh, Jim Brown, Johnny Unitas, O. J. Simpson, and Dan Marino are frequently championed as having been the best. Walter Payton is the best football player of all time, wrote Hub Arkush in *Pro Football Weekly*. Payton won an NBC pre-game show call-in poll (as best running back of all time) over Jim Brown, O. J. Simpson, and Gale Sayers, all of whom were present on-camera as viewers dialed the 900 number. Insofar as Vince Lombardi's Green Bay Packers of the early 1960s are often deemed the best team ever, Bart Starr and Paul Hornung are popular choices. (Lombardi is supposed to have said that Forrest Gregg was the best player he ever coached.) The Super Bowl is often good for best-player-of-all-time pronouncements. "I don't know what else Joe Montana has to do to prove that he's the greatest player to ever play this game," Cincinnati receiver Chris Collinsworth said after Bowl XXIII. Even George Blanda has his partisans. His perpetual-calendar-busting career allowed him to rack up 2,002 points. No one else stuck around long enough to do that. They all had other things to do.

In no other major sport has the role of the individual player changed so much over the past few decades. Way back when, pro football was more like the high school game. Pro players of the 1940s played offense when their team had the ball, and defense when it didn't. Versatility was a necessary virtue. Then, like the dinosaurs, football became big and specialized. In the two-platoon modern game, players play one phase of the game very well and others not at all. To compete in today's game, a player requires near-optimum height and build for his position.

This distorts the statistics. Under the old system players couldn't play the full 60 minutes. They had to spend some time on the bench catching their breath. Since they didn't play full-time, cumulative statistics were lower.

Football has changed in other ways, too. Stadiums are enclosed. It's easier to run on Astroturf than on grass. The players have gotten bigger while the field has stayed the same size: The spaces between linemen have shrunk. Expansion teams have tripled the number of pro players. Presumably that means the talent is diluted. Or does it? Football has become more popular and better paid relative to other sports in the past few decades. It might attract more talent than it used to, so the significance of the expansion teams depends on what point you're trying to make.

As before, let's agree to look for someone's best season ever. (The best-career approach is less attractive in football since some of the candidates for best player are still playing.) "Best season" will be defined by how much a player contributed to victory per time unit. What should the time unit be? Although the down might seem analogous to the out in baseball, it's not. Barring a tie, the number of outs is fixed. The number of downs varies. The unrenewable resource in football is the time on the clock, the 60 minutes of football time (up to three hours of real time) in which the teams have to score. Football accomplishments should be expressed per minute or per game. Stating records per season leads to confusion. The number of games a season has varied from 10 to 16, not counting seasons in which there have been strikes.

The hard part is deciding who contributes what to a team's victory. Even in the old days, it was comparing apples with oranges. The platoon system has made players and their skills all the more incommensurable. Football is more strictly a team game than the other major sports. A star baseball player can score runs even if he's on the worst team of all time. A good football player can't do much unless he is backed with good teammates.

The first hurdle we have to leap is that not all positions are equally well covered by the statistics. There are no meaningful individual statistics on blocking linemen's contributions, for instance. Linemen are important mainly in a collective sense. A line is defined more by its weakest points than by one exceptional lineman's strength.

Let's take as an axiom that the most important individual contributions *are* reflected in the statistics. The offensive players who pass, receive, rush, and score points—and thus get statistical credit for it—are more important than those players who contribute more anonymously. If the positions that are slighted by statistics were all that important, there would be individual statistics for them.

You don't have to agree with this, but if you don't, there is no hope of deciding who is the best football player from statistics.

What statistics do we use? A team has to score points to win. It's an often-quoted fact that the player who scored the most points in a single year is Paul Hornung. As halfback for Green Bay in 1960, he scored 176 points (as 15 touchdowns, 15 field goals, and 41 PATs). Hornung's record is comfortably higher than the number-two point leader, Mark Moseley of Washington (1983), who scored 161 points. These records should really be recalculated as points per game. Doing so only increases Hornung's lead. Green Bay played 12 games in 1960, meaning that Hornung averaged 14.7 points a game. Moseley's 161 points were spread out over 16 games for an average of 10.1 points a game.

Yet this doesn't prove that Hornung was the best player ever. Hornung scored more than half of the points Green Bay scored that year. Good as he was, he didn't contribute half the total team effort. Any attempt to decide which position is most important must account for the fact that some important players, such as the quarterback, score few or no points.

Football's lingua franca is yards. Passing skills may be incomparably different from rushing skills, but yards from all types of plays go into the same bin. A team that has progressed to their opponents' 5-yard line stands a high chance of scoring, *and it doesn't matter how they got there.*

The best football player ought to be the one responsible for gaining the most yards per game. This definition isn't perfect. Some contributions aren't reflected in yardage statistics. Some gains of yardage don't count for anything. Nonetheless, yardage is quantitative and simple. It's a way of comparing rushing with passing with receiving with kicking.

The conventional statistics were designed to compare like skills: Jerry Rice's receiving with Dwight Clark's receiving; O. J. Simpson's rushing with Walter Payton's rushing. They give undivided credit for all yards gained. Of course that's wrong. The offensive linemen help and deserve some of the credit. Maybe the coach deserves credit.

We're mainly interested in comparing passing and receiving yardage with rushing yardage. So we'll ignore the contributions of offensive linemen and assume that a rusher is 100 percent responsible for his credited yardage. A rusher who makes a 15-yard rush contributes as much to his team as the *two* players who make a 15-yard pass. The NFL statistics duplicate yardage on passing plays. A player who throws a 15-yard pass gets credit for 15 yards. The player who catches the pass also gets credit for the same 15 yards. Their team has gained only 15 yards, not 30. That means the credit for a completed pass must be split between the passer and the receiver. We want to say something like the passer and the receiver were responsible for 7 1/2 yards each.

Should passing credit be split 50-50 between passer and receiver? The only realistic answer is: It depends. It's tougher to throw a long pass than a short one. It's not necessarily harder to catch a long pass, but a long pass demands that the receiver do a lot of running through enemy territory. Loosely speaking, things tend to even out. In the absence of a compelling argument to the contrary, let's assume that in general passers and receivers share equal responsibility for passing yardage.

The next step is to convert yards into points. The usual coaching guesstimate is that a gain of about 12 yards is worth 1 point. The rationale goes like this: A touchdown is worth 6 points. The team receiving the kickoff generally starts with the ball around its 25- or 30-yard line. It has to advance the ball 70 or 75 yards to make a touchdown.

The logical way to rate players is by points per game. Take the total season yardage that a player was responsible for (100 percent of rushing yardage; 50 percent of passing and receiving yardage). Divide by 12 to get the number of points he created. Divide that by the number of games in the season to get points per game.

Then we can say that when Walter Payton rushed for 1,852 yards in 1977, he produced the equivalent of 154 points for Chicago. There were 14 games in the 1977 season, so Payton gets credit for 11.0 points per game.

Some yards are worth more than a twelfth of a point. Suppose a team makes it to their opponents' 1-yard line. At that point the touchdown is extremely likely. The player who actually does the honors doesn't deserve credit for the 6 points (unless he was also responsible for getting to the 1-yard line in the first place). The touchdown's 6 points has already been factored into the estimate of 12 yards to the point.

Not that the touchdown itself is worth nothing. Even from one millimeter shy of the goal line, a touchdown is not a foregone conclusion. The likelihood of a point-blank touchdown is something like 80 percent. Making the touchdown also makes the team eligible for a point-after, which hardly anyone misses. Let's say that the touchdown alone is worth about a point (for the PAT). That means that a typical drive from a team's 28-yard line to the opponents' goal is worth 6 points for yardage plus one for the touchdown: 7 points, which is exactly what the team would normally score.

In 1977 Walter Payton made 14 touchdowns in as many games. Awarding him an extra point for each of the touchdowns raises his effective contribution to 12.0 points per game.

Interception statistics can refine our estimate of a passer's value to his team. Each interception causes the team to lose possession of the ball and therefore costs it points. How many?

Well, the *worst* thing that can happen is for your opponents to make a touchdown and a point-after. Your team would slip 7 points relative to the other team. Then your team would start back from square one with the opponents kicking off to you.

The *best* thing that could happen, within reason, would be for your opponents to fumble the ball right back to you. On the average, a turnover must be somewhere between these two extremes.

Coaches assume a turnover costs about 4 points—the better part of a touchdown and point-after. To see why, picture the simple case where the turnover occurs on your 1-yard line. Then the opposing team is a cinch to make the touchdown and point-after. Assume as above that that high probability is worth 6 points. After that, they would kick off to your team. *In effect, that advances your team from the 1-yard line to about the 25-yard line.* An advance of 24 yards is worth about 2 points. On the debit side are 6 points for the likely scoring, but on the credit side there are 2 points for the probable advance. The net damage is about 4 points.

Similar reasoning shows that the effect of a turnover is roughly the same anywhere on the field. When your team is close to the goal and about to score, the turnover is mitigated by the fact that your opponents will be a long way from scoring. You're likely to lose some yardage but not everything. When you're near your own team's goal and aren't sacrificing much of a chance of scoring, your opponents *are* likely to score. The chance of your opponents scoring the touchdown is never *that* great unless your team was in a bad way to start with. The turnover is never as bad as giving up a full touchdown. Hence the 4 points estimate.

In 1984 Dan Marino's passes gained 5,084 yards for Miami. At 12 yards a point, that's the equivalent of 424 points. A record 48 passes scored touchdowns. Awarding a bonus point for each raises the total to 472 points. Marino also threw 17 intercepted passes. Debiting 4 points for each (68 points lost) leaves 404 points for the season. Both the credits for the yards and touchdowns and the debits for the interceptions should be shared with the receivers, or intended receivers, as the case may be. Giving Marino 50 percent credit leaves him 202 points. Finally, dividing this by the schedule of 16 games gives an estimate of Marino's real worth to Miami as 12.6 points a game.

Impressive as that is, it just misses being the best season of all time by points per game. In 1973 O. J. Simpson rushed for 2,003 yards and made 12 touchdowns. That's the equivalent of 179 points, and since it was rushing, Simpson shares the primary credit with no one. There were 14 scheduled games in 1973, so Simpson averaged 12.8 points a game. That is the highest of any player/season.

The NFL statistics do not tell us everything. They list interceptions by passer but not by would-be receiver. The degree of "fault" for a failed pass varies. Sometimes it's the passer's fault, and sometimes it's the receiver's. Other times, it's more a matter of a great interception by the other team. We can probably do no better than to assume as above that the debits for interceptions should be shared equally by passer and intended receiver. But we don't know the intended receivers, at least not from the NFL statistics. Consequently we aren't able to deduct 50 percent of 4 points each time a receiver failed to complete a pass.

Fortunately, this won't make any difference in deciding the

most valuable player of all. The best passers always produce more yardage than the best receivers. Based on yardage and touchdowns, the best receiver of all time was Elroy Hirsch in the 1951 season. His pass receptions totaled 1,495 yards, and 17 were touchdowns. Had Hirsch not been responsible for a single interception, he would have been worth about 5.9 points a game to the Rams (at 50 percent credit for completed passes). That's far, far behind Simpson, Marino, and dozens of other rushers and passers. All told, Hirsch's 1951 season would rank about 36th in effective points per game.

It is premature to name Simpson the best football player of all time. Points have not been equally valuable at all times through pro football history. We should compare these points-per-game figures with the average points scored that year.

A graph of the average points scored per team per game in the NFL shows two features. From 1935 to about 1948 it rises dramatically from 11 to 23 points a game. After 1948 it levels off, varying erratically from year to year. From 1948 to the present, the average has been about 21 points a game. A modest dip in the 1970s plunged to 17 points a game in 1977. (The points scored in the AFL was never more than a point or two different from the NFL average of the same year.)

That means that a point scored in 1935 was worth almost twice what one scored more recently would be. To put things in perspective, let's divide the number of points a player was responsible for by the average number of points scored by an NFL team in a game that same year. The table shows the top players of the post-1935 era ranked by this normalized figure (last column).

| | Year | Position | Yards | TDs | Int. | Games | Pts./ Game | % Credit | Credited Pts./ Game | NFL Avg. Pts./ Game | % of Avg. Pts. |
|---|---|---|---|---|---|---|---|---|---|---|---|
| Walter Payton | 1977 | Rusher | 1,852 | 14 | | 14 | 12.0 | 100 | 12.0 | 17.0 | 70.7 |
| O. J. Simpson | 1973 | Rusher | 2,003 | 12 | | 14 | 12.8 | 100 | 12.8 | 19.0 | 67.3 |
| Dan Marino | 1984 | Passer | 5,084 | 48 | 17 | 16 | 25.2 | 50 | 12.6 | 21.0 | 60.1 |
| O. J. Simpson | 1975 | Rusher | 1,817 | 16 | | 14 | 12.0 | 100 | 12.0 | 21.0 | 56.9 |
| Eric Dickerson | 1984 | Rusher | 2,105 | 14 | | 16 | 11.8 | 100 | 11.8 | 21.0 | 56.4 |
| Earl Campbell | 1980 | Rusher | 1,934 | 13 | | 16 | 10.9 | 100 | 10.9 | 20.0 | 54.4 |
| Jim Brown | 1963 | Rusher | 1,863 | 12 | | 14 | 11.9 | 100 | 11.9 | 22.0 | 54.3 |
| Jim Brown | 1958 | Rusher | 1,527 | 17 | | 12 | 12.0 | 100 | 12.0 | 23.0 | 52.3 |
| Earl Campbell | 1979 | Rusher | 1,697 | 19 | | 16 | 10.0 | 100 | 10.0 | 20.0 | 50.1 |
| Otis Armstrong | 1974 | Rusher | 1,407 | 9 | | 14 | 9.0 | 100 | 9.0 | 18.0 | 50.1 |
| O. J. Simpson | 1976 | Rusher | 1,503 | 8 | | 14 | 9.5 | 100 | 9.5 | 19.0 | 50.1 |
| Jim Brown | 1959 | Rusher | 1,329 | 14 | | 12 | 10.4 | 100 | 10.4 | 21.0 | 49.5 |
| Eric Dickerson | 1986 | Rusher | 1,821 | 11 | | 16 | 10.2 | 100 | 10.2 | 21.0 | 48.4 |
| Eric Dickerson | 1983 | Rusher | 1,808 | 18 | | 16 | 10.5 | 100 | 10.5 | 22.0 | 47.9 |
| Bert Jones | 1976 | Passer | 3,104 | 24 | 9 | 14 | 17.6 | 50 | 8.8 | 19.0 | 46.4 |
| Jim Taylor | 1962 | Rusher | 1,474 | 19 | | 14 | 10.1 | 100 | 10.1 | 22.0 | 46.0 |
| George Rogers | 1981 | Rusher | 1,674 | 13 | | 16 | 9.5 | 100 | 9.5 | 21.0 | 45.4 |
| Jim Brown | 1965 | Rusher | 1,544 | 17 | | 14 | 10.4 | 100 | 10.4 | 23.0 | 45.2 |
| Marcus Allen | 1985 | Rusher | 1,759 | 11 | | 16 | 9.8 | 100 | 9.8 | 22.0 | 44.8 |
| Spec Sanders | 1947 | Rusher | 1,432 | 18 | | 14 | 9.8 | 100 | 9.8 | 22.0 | 44.6 |

| | Year | Position | Yards | TDs | Int. | Games | Pts./ Game | % Credit | Credited Pts./ Game | NFL Avg. Pts./ Game | % of Avg. Pts. |
|---|---|---|---|---|---|---|---|---|---|---|---|
| Rick Casares | 1956 | Rusher | 1,126 | 12 | | 12 | 8.8 | 100 | 8.8 | 20.0 | 44.1 |
| Jim Brown | 1960 | Rusher | 1,257 | 9 | | 12 | 9.5 | 100 | 9.5 | 22.0 | 43.1 |
| Jim Nance | 1966 | Rusher | 1,458 | 11 | | 14 | 9.5 | 100 | 9.5 | 22.0 | 43.0 |
| Sid Luckman | 1943 | Passer | 2,194 | 28 | 12 | 10 | 16.3 | 50 | 8.1 | 19.0 | 42.9 |
| Jim Brown | 1964 | Rusher | 1,446 | 7 | | 14 | 9.1 | 100 | 9.1 | 22.0 | 41.4 |
| Jim Brown | 1961 | Rusher | 1,408 | 8 | | 14 | 9.0 | 100 | 9.0 | 22.0 | 40.7 |
| Leroy Kelly | 1968 | Rusher | 1,239 | 16 | | 14 | 8.5 | 100 | 8.5 | 21.0 | 40.6 |
| Steve Van Buren | 1949 | Rusher | 1,146 | 11 | | 12 | 8.9 | 100 | 8.9 | 22.0 | 40.3 |
| Otto Graham | 1949 | Passer | 2,785 | 19 | 10 | 12 | 17.6 | 50 | 8.8 | 22.0 | 40.0 |

Measured this way, the best player of all time is Walter Payton—his 1977 season. Simpson, Marino, and Jim Brown matched or bettered Payton's 12.0 credited points per game, but Payton scored those 12 points a game at the bottom of the 1970s scoring slump. For whatever reason, it was harder to score points then than in Marino's or Simpson's salad days. Points were more "expensive," and every one was more likely to make the difference between victory and defeat. Payton's 12.0 points per game was 70.7 percent of what an average NFL team scored in 1977.

Now let's step back a moment. Figures are all well and fine. Is there anything that might lead us to reconsider the conclusion that Payton is the best player?

The main hitch in all this reasoning is the division of credit for passing yardage. Fifty percent was pulled out of the air as a reasonable guess. Reasonable it is, but it could well be off. It could be off enough to upset Payton's lead and make Marino the most valuable player of all time. We should ask whether, in the specific case of Marino and his pass receivers in 1984, Marino deserved more than 50 percent credit for his passes.

When a star passer throws to a middling receiver, it's natural to assume—rightly or not—that the passer was mostly responsible. Mark Clayton and Mark Duper caught the lion's share of Marino's passes. Undeniably talented, neither ranks nearly as high in the pantheon of receivers as Marino does among passers. Despite all the passes Marino was shooting, neither Clayton nor Duper was the top receiver for 1984 (it was Roy Green of St. Louis).

There are those who downplay Marino's 1984 record, particularly the unprecedented 48 touchdowns. They say it was a fluke of Miami's pass-intensive strategy, and that the credit must be shared with his teammates. Both points have some merit. Marino wouldn't have made so many passes if the Dolphins hadn't concentrated on passing. Conversely, Miami wouldn't have tried to pass so much if it hadn't had such a talented passer in Marino. Everyone who scores touchdowns does so with a lot of help. There does not seem to be any particular reason to think that Marino got more of this help than anyone else.

Marino was a quarterback. Payton wasn't. Although it is fashionable to say that too much is made of the quarterback's strategic role, a good quarterback is probably worth *something* beyond his passing—especially when a team has a 14-2-0 season as Miami did in 1984.

It comes down to this. With some confidence we can assert that the best football player/season of all time is either Walter Payton (1977) or Dan Marino (1984). If you think that Marino should get about 59 percent or more of the credit for his passing yardage in 1984 (relative to the nominal 100 percent credit a rusher gets), then the best player of all time is Marino. If you think Marino deserves less than 59 percent, then rusher Walter Payton's 1977 season is tops. It's questionable if anyone, including Marino and his pass receivers, knows how much credit Marino should get.

# THE MOST INGENIOUS COLLEGE PRANK

# JUDGING
# HOW *FUNNY*

a college prank was is difficult. Most are of the you-had-to-be-there type. Ingenuity is more open to comparison. Some pranks produce more social distortion per man-hour expended. However, anyone asking what is the most successful prank ever must confront the fact that many of the "best" pranks never occurred. Either they're complete fabrications or they have been embellished outrageously in the retelling. Obviously, only real events count. We attempted to confirm stories of pranks from back issues of local and student newspapers and via college information offices.

A widespread prank (everyone thinks it was original at his school) is the fictitious student. A real student fills out a spare application and enrolls a fake student under a made-up name that is just jokey enough to be believable (e.g., "Joseph Oznot," Princeton class of '68). With the aid of classmates, the mythical student takes tests, signs petitions, sends huffy letters to the local newspaper, gets paged at sporting events, sends the dean gift subscriptions to girlie magazines, etc., etc. The logical denouement is having the fake student graduate with honors—or so the stories go.

By 1940, the Atlanta *Journal* could run an article on this prank as something of an ivy-covered tradition, mentioning a "Tom Lambert" who attended—that is, didn't attend—St. Petersburg Junior College, and a pair of fictitious students, "Joe Gish" and "W. T. Door," at the Naval Academy. Priority appears to go to "George P. Burdell" of Georgia Tech, whom the article dates to circa 1926 (1920 is mentioned elsewhere, and 1927 is more likely).

By more romantic accounts, Burdell's inventor died of cancer about three years after graduation. In fact, a middle-aged alumnus named Ed Smith finally confessed to creating Burdell in a 1977 article in the Atlanta *Journal & Constitution Magazine.* Smith said Burdell was named after Burdell, his cat, and George P. Butler, a principal of the prep school he attended.

The Burdell prank is the masterwork of its kind. If signing up a guy for one class is good, then signing him up for two classes is twice as good, and signing him up for every class in the college catalogue is as boss as you can get. Someone did that during Georgia Tech's 1969 spring registration. Georgia Tech had just computerized its registration system, and some well-meaning higher-up commented that it would be well-nigh impossible for students to enroll mythical persons the way they had with the old-fashioned system. George P. Burdell signed up for 3,000 hours of study that quarter. Eighteen hours is average.

Burdell quickly evolved into a self-perpetuating mythos that transcended the efforts of Smith and his friends. Burdell's name became carte blanche to free magazines (subscribe under Burdell's name and don't pay; most publishers send several months' worth of issues before halting the subscription). Clips in the Georgia Tech information office also describe Burdell's use in the once popular sport of campus insurance agent baiting. ("You ought to see George Burdell. That rich kid will buy anything!")

At some point students discovered that the society columns of Atlanta newspapers will print just about anything that looks all right without checking. Soon Burdell was throwing glittering fetes for promising debutantes at the Piedmont Driving Club. The papers belatedly caught on and blacklisted him. The tenure of society editors being what it is, Burdell has staged several social comebacks. A March 14, 1971, notice in the Atlanta *Journal & Constitution* had a Mr. and Mrs. George P. Burdell betrothing George Jr. to Constance E. Crane, a socially prominent young astronomer. Days later, after any number of Tech grads had pointed out the gaffe, the paper ran a retraction. The senior society editor said she had let the notice pass because she had in her time seen and run legitimate notices on people named Robin Hood, Perry Mason, and Robert E. Lee, all living in the Atlanta area.

In some colleges, in some programs, it is barely conceivable that a student could pass all the tests, accumulate necessary credits, and qualify for a diploma without any faculty contact. There does not seem to be any instance of this happening, though. Burdell's "graduation" was a case of officialdom going along with the joke. That's just not the same thing. The Georgia Tech alumni roster and other publications have variously listed George P. Burdell as a 1930 or 1970 bachelor of science.

Of course, even by 1930 the joke was ancient history to everyone concerned. The Atlanta *Constitution* claimed (in an article about the prank) that Burdell was accepted into Harvard, presumably for postgraduate work. Stories of Burdell being appointed Regents Professor and Dean of Humanities and Fine Arts stem from a letter published in the Atlanta *Constitution* (November 16, 1971), in which the writer, "Burdell," claims to hold that position (along with having received a Ph.D. in 1960). Georgia Tech says it *has* gotten requests for Burdell's transcripts from potential employers.

The Burdell prank is successful for several reasons. A prank that creates an odd reversal of the usual state of affairs is better than one that is merely malicious. And, all other things being equal, a prank with a large audience is more successful than one with a smaller audience. Burdell has become a permanent Georgia Tech fixture. He is still being used as a handy scapegoat today, meaning that he has been in continuous existence over sixty years. The effective audience for the prank is something like sixty times the size of the Georgia Tech incoming class, plus the readership of the Atlanta *Journal & Constitution:* roughly, $60 \times 2,900 + 440,000$, or about 600,000.

The antiphon to the bogus person is the fake nullification of a real person. In 1942 students at New York University's Bronx campus falsely reported the death of Dean William Bush Baer to *The New York Times.* Baer's demise rated $7\frac{1}{4}$ column inches in the May 9 issue. The obituary is a matter of public record. It is further claimed, though it sounds too good to be true, that Baer came to work to find the flag at half-staff and the chapel choir singing dirges. The retraction (2¼ column inches) of the following day did not identify the culprit: "The New York Times, which was imposed upon, regrets the error and any concern it may have caused Dean Baer, his relatives and friends." The perpetrators were believed to be students upset over exams.

There have been similar pranks elsewhere, but this one stands out for getting the obit in the nation's paper of record. Georgia Tech's Burdell does not seem to have cracked the New York society pages. (Audience size = 1942 Saturday circulation of *The New York Times:* about 500,000.)

Caltech is acknowledged as a prank capital. The techie-nerd mentality excels in practical jokes that, while not exactly funny, succeed on cleverness. A pair of Caltech pranks of the early 1970s faked not merely death but nonexistence. In 1970 Bruce Ault ('70), Dana Powers ('70), Ron Horn ('73), and Chip Smith (faculty, physics department) entered the Spaulding Laboratory parking lot one night and eradicated the parking space of an unpopular administrator in the chemistry department. They repainted the lines and names designating the reserved spaces, making each space just a little wider and leaving out the spot reserved for the victim's Mercury Cougar.

There's also a nice existential edge to the missing-room prank of 1972. While Caltech frosh Chuck Conner ('75) took a week off from studies to visit a girlfriend, dorm mates took the liberty of annihilating all physical traces of his existence on this earth. They plastered over the door to his room, and moved a lighting fixture to the newly blank wall, so that Conner would appear all the more deluded in insisting a door had been there.

When the victim returned, his dorm mates could not recall having ever met him.

Hoaxes frequently entail a student being killed in front of his classmates. In April 1925, more than 75 gullible Dartmouth students showed up for an announced duel between students F. B. Wallis ('25) and F. J. Wolski (apparently a fictitious identity). Principals and seconds drove off in a car. Shortly afterward, four shots were heard. The mob of would-be witnesses ran to look for the bodies but found none.

Possibly the most famous Dartmouth prank was an impersonation. According to *The Dartmouth*, the student newspaper, it was the work of the paper's retiring editors. Herbert Dobbins, a theatrical character actor who had appeared in *Abie's Irish Rose*, was hired to impersonate "Nelson Billings," a fictitious millionaire planning a generous bequest to the college. The hoaxers convinced Dartmouth to organize a reception for the benefactor, complete with state police escort, cannon salute, and band concert. Dobbins addressed the assembly with an "impromptu" speech written by playwright Valentine Davies. Dobbins revealed that his son had planned to go to Dartmouth but had died and that he wanted to make a gift in his honor. "So therefore, in memory of my son Nelson Billings III, I present to Dartmouth College the 1934 football team." Onstage came a team of five unemployed farmers and three students made up as bums in old football uniforms. The perpetrators claimed credit with a large sign dropped from a nearby window. The gibe at Dartmouth's poor gridiron showing does not come off funny in the retelling, but it rates something for miseen-scène. According to *The Dartmouth,* the only hitches were a cannon backfire (one slight injury) and that Dobbins mistakenly mentioned the 1933 rather than the 1934 football team. (Dartmouth enrollment: about 5,000.)

Attempts to nail down the date and circumstances of a much-repeated suicide hoax failed, suggesting that it may never have happened. Supposedly, a student walked into a notoriously difficult final exam and feigned taking the test. Near the end of the allotted time he jumped up, screamed he couldn't take it anymore, and leapt out the window. Accomplices had a net somewhere below. This is claimed to have happened at several schools.

Putting things where they don't belong—especially putting livestock where they don't belong—is a popular category of prank. Dartmouth students had put a live cow in the campus chapel, and possibly other incongruous places, by the turn of the century. The thing to remember in comparing bovine stunts is that cows spook around stairs, greatly increasing the challenge of vertical cow displacement. Priority for getting a cow at least one story off the ground appears to go to a group of MIT students. They got "Maisie," a heifer, on the roof of a dormitory in 1928. Getting the cow up and down required Pavlovian reinforcement in the form of grass and water at each landing. The claims of a cow on top of MIT's 149-foot-high Great Dome result from the confusion of this prank with a 1979 reprise. The later prank put a fiberglass cow, stolen from an area restaurant, on top of the dome. Anyone who has dealt with irritable livestock will tell you that's not even in the same league. The best MIT dome stunt, incidentally, was the placing of a working phone booth on the dome. As phone company workers scaled the dome to retrieve it, someone dialed the number to have the phone ring. (MIT enrollment: about 10,000).

A prominent Georgia Tech flagpole was topped with an eagle statuette. One day, a cage mysteriously appeared around the eagle. This typifies the conceptual prank: no big deal until you wonder how someone scaled the flagpole. (The workman sent to retrieve the cage found a note saying, "George P. Burdell was here.") The parties responsible used neither ladders nor cherry pickers. The cage had been lifted with a helium weather balloon. The balloon was attached to the cage with slipknots, the string running to the perpetrators on the ground. They guided the cage into place over the bird, then tugged on the string to release the knots. The balloon headed for the stratosphere, pulling the strings with it.

Caltech's "orange cannon" of the 1950s falls into the things-where-they-don't-belong genre. It is another case of what might have been a mere technical hack being used to create a surreal effect. Students constructed a pneumatic cannon capable of propelling an orange from Caltech's Ricketts Court across several blocks of torpidly bourgeois Pasadena. Every day at the strike of noon, an orange dropped from the sky onto the campus of neighboring Pasadena City College. Eventually people at PCC started wondering where the oranges were coming from. The *Pasadena Star-News* ran an article on the mystery, and Caltech students advanced the theory that the oranges were coming from outer space. (Enrollment of Pasadena City

College + circulation of *Pasadena Star-News* = 20,000 + 39,000 = 59,000.)

Most varieties of campus sabotage (turning off the lights at an inopportune moment, computer tampering, etc.) raise shrugs. Robert Morris's 1988 UNIX computer virus probably doesn't qualify as a prank—not so much because it caused real hardship, which admittedly some bona fide pranks do, but because it wasn't intended to be funny. (Employment at eleven computer centers affected: approximately 50,000.)

One sabotage prank claimed to have happened several times at Penn State rises a bit above the pack for resourcefulness. The Old Main's bell rings every hour and is regarded as a picturesque nuisance. Students have taken advantage of the winter cold to silence it by turning the bell upside down and filling it with water. By morning the clapper is immobilized in ice. (Penn State enrollment = 3,400.)

Creative modifications of school mascots or public landmarks are abundant. A well-known but relatively weak prank is MIT's measurement of the Harvard Bridge using underclassman Oliver Smoot ('62). Fraternity pledges were assigned the project of measuring the Harvard Bridge. For this task they used a semi-acquiescent Smoot as a yardstick. They set him down at one end of the bridge, painted a mark at his head, picked him up and moved him forward so his feet matched the mark, and painted another mark at his head. They kept doing this and concluded that the bridge was 364.4 Smoots plus one ear long. This would have been forgotten long ago if not for the tireless efforts of Lambda Chi Alpha to repaint the Smoot marks when road workers try to eradicate them. Today police use the marks to pinpoint the location of accidents. (Audience: something on the order of the population of Boston, 560,000.) Possibly more amusing is a 1937 Caltech determination of the distance to Pasadena City Hall as 5,678 dead mackerels.

As mascot stunts go, none is as inspired as UCLA's kidnapping of the USC football team's dog mascot, George Tirebiter. They shaved the dog's coat so that it said UCLA. The dog wore a sweater to the Rose Bowl.

Sheer number of people affected by a prank isn't everything. It is something, and it is one way of winnowing out the more successful pranks. It is a rare collegiate prank that directly affects half a million unwitting people. Georgia Tech's fake student and NYU's faked death of Dean Baer each had an audience of about half a million, mostly via newspapers. Considerations of audience size for pranks quickly leads to Caltech's three nationally televised Rose Bowl pranks. Each had an audience of about sixty times the Georgia Tech and NYU pranks.

The most successful of the pranks, and defensibly the best college prank of all time, is the first, the Rose Bowl card stunt of 1961. It is good because the target is the essentially vacuous institution of cheerleading, and it maximized public exposure to a degree possible only in the age of television. "It has emerged as the standard against which all other pranks are compared, and has never been equalled, let alone surpassed," states the Alumni Association's *Legends of Caltech* (1982).

A group of fourteen Lloyd House students spending the winter holidays on campus were inspired by newspaper accounts describing the two Rose Bowl teams, the University of Washington Huskies and the University of Minnesota Gophers. The scheduled halftime entertainment included an elaborate set of "card stunts" (where a mass of cheerleaders form words or pictures by holding colored cards over their heads). Someone got the idea of changing the instructions so that the stunt would spell out a message of Caltech's choosing.

Varying accounts of the prank appeared in the press. The following version is attested to by several of the perpetrators. A young-looking Caltech student posed as a reporter for a high school student newspaper. He interviewed the University of Washington's head cheerleader. The Caltech student feigned interest in the details of the process, and the cheerleader explained it, mentioning that the instructions and master sheets were kept in a satchel under one of the cheerleader's beds. It was also ascertained, in passing, that the cheerleaders would spend New Year's Eve at Disneyland.

The halftime entertainment was to include fifteen card stunts. The cheerleaders would successively depict a salute to science (theme of the Seattle World's Fair), a Husky (the team mascot), the word "Washington," and an American flag. Each cheerleader was supplied with a set of colored cards. A given color could be required several times in the course of the stunt. Rather than stack each cheerleader's cards in order, each cheerleader was given an instruction list. The instructions, different for each cheerleader, told him what card to display for each stunt. To create animation effects, such as a word being written from left to right, the instructions had cheerleaders wait for a numerical cue (dictated by megaphone) to switch colors in the middle of a stunt. It follows that no cheerleader had any way of knowing what massed effect his card would make. Nor did the cheerleaders memorize their instructions (which changed from game to game). They followed the instruction cards. The cards themselves were prepared from gridded sketches of the desired effects.

While the cheerleaders were at dinner, Caltech students picked the lock to their rooms and stole one of the 2,232 instructions cards. This was taken to a printer to duplicate in mass.

The next step was to prepare new master plans. The old sketches were set out on Lloyd House's dining tables. New grids of 2,232 squares were drawn up, and new pictures built up square by square with colored stamps. To get the maximum effect, they kept the modifications subtle until near the end of the stunt sequence. On the early stunts, the only changes were minor aesthetic improvements (rounding the corners of an Erlenmeyer flask in the salute to science, for instance). Stunts 12 through 14 were changed completely. The Lloyd House residents entered the new instructions on the cards, and replaced them in the satchel in the cheerleaders' room (the occupants still at Disneyland). One security leak threatened the plot. A Minnesota student, a guest of one of the helpers, was shocked to learn of the subterfuge. Fortunately, the joke was mainly at the expense of Washington, Minnesota's rival, so she vowed silence.

The card stunt was to be seen by approximately 30 million people on NBC television. The first eleven stunts went as planned, incorporating Lloyd House's slight but telling modifications. Stunt 12 showed a beaver, symbol of Caltech. TV announcers dutifully pronounced the misshapen beast a Washington Husky.

Stunt 13 was supposed to spell out "Washington" in a flowing hand from left to right. It actually spelled it out from right to left. This tame modification was true artistry. Only the head cheerleader, calling the signals from his megaphone, would realize that something was wrong.

Stunt 14 was the payoff. The cards spelled out "CALTECH" in bold black letters on a white background. The TV announcers were aghast. (Allegedly, one speculated that as part of the tribute to science Washington was saluting Pasadena's well-known technical school.) After that, the head cheerleader cut his losses and ordered the band off the field. Though Washington didn't know it, the final card stunt of an American flag was unchanged.

This prank was far superior to an abortive 1981 attempt to inflate a buried balloon during the game, and the derivative 1984 rigging of the Rose Bowl scoreboard. In the 1984 Rose Bowl incident, two Caltech students contrived a radio control that could usurp the electronic scoreboard from two miles away. During the fourth quarter of the UCLA-Illinois match, the pranksters changed the matrix readout to "Caltech 38 MIT 9." Horrified officials pulled the plug before they could display several other gibes, including "Caltech 2 Rose Bowl 0." Although the TV audience was probably a bit greater, the '84 stunt lacked the winning simplicity of its predecessor. Jimmying the card instructions has more flair because it's simpler. And the scoreboard stunt prankster didn't get away with it. Despite a generally tolerant public reaction, the Pasadena city prosecutor saw nothing funny in the prank. The two students ended up paying $330 in damages. The 1961 pranksters were never indicted.

# SEVEN

# THE MOST DIFFICULT TONGUE TWISTER

# THE
# GUINNESS BOOK

*of World Records* cites the claim of Ken Parkin of Teesside, England, that the hardest English tongue twister is:

*The sixth sick sheik's sixth sheep's sick.*

We compiled a list containing this and other allegedly difficult tongue twisters and asked volunteers to recite them. They were required to read each sentence or phrase quickly in a regular reading voice. Each volunteer was allowed to read the list silently before beginning, but no "practice" elocutions were permitted. A judge ruled on whether each attempt was successful. Where, in the opinion of our judge, it was felt that a volunteer had not repeated a phrase quickly enough, the result was disallowed and he was asked to try again. Only flawless enunciations counted.

The list included two easy ones, "Peter Piper" (the lengthy version) and "She sells seashells," for comparison purposes. It spanned the genre's variety, from tongue twisters proper to a phrase difficult to say five times fast. The list went:

*Better baby buggy bumpers.*

*Three new blue beans in a new-blown bladder.*

*The Leith police dismisseth us.*

*Peter Piper picked a peck of pickled pepper; a peck of
pickled pepper Peter Piper picked. If Peter Piper picked
a peck of pickled pepper, where is the peck of pickled
pepper Peter Piper picked?*

*The seething sea ceaseth and thus the seething sea
sufficeth us.*

*She sells seashells by the seashore.*

*The sixth sick sheik's sixth sheep's sick.*

*Sixty-six sick chicks.*

*Long slim slick sycamore saplings.*

*Tie twine to three tree twigs*

*Toy boat* (said five times fast)

*Twixt six thick thumbs stick six thick sticks.*

*How much wood could a woodchuck chuck if a woodchuck
could chuck wood?*

The percentage of successful attempts (out of 30 total attempts) was computed for each tongue twister. "Seething sea" and "Sheik" were so far out in front that their lead was never in doubt. They were the only tongue twisters that most volunteers muffed on most attempts.

| | Success Rate | Words | Rate/Word |
|---|---|---|---|
| Seething | 3% | 11 | 73% |
| Sheik | 30% | 7 | 84% |
| Leith police | 67% | 5 | 92% |
| Chicks | 77% | 4 | 94% |
| Toy boat | 67% | 10 | 96% |
| Twigs | 80% | 6 | 96% |
| Seashells | 83% | 6 | 97% |
| Sycamore | 87% | 5 | 97% |
| Woodchuck | 80% | 13 | 98% |
| Peter Piper | 57% | 35 | 98% |
| Beans | 90% | 9 | 99% |
| Thumbs | 93% | 8 | 99% |
| Bumpers | 97% | 4 | 99% |

The errors were fairly consistent with each tongue twister. With "Sheik" and "Chicks," the problem was saying the wrong word, such as "sixty-sick six chicks" or "sick sixth sheik." Possibly "Seashells" and "Peter Piper" were easier because most of the speakers were familiar with them. On the other hand, most volunteers stumbled on the second "woodchuck" in that familiar twister.

"S" sounds are the richest source of material for hard twisters. They can be hard even without alliteration. "Seething sea" may derive from a biblical sentence:

Philip saith unto him, "Lord, show us the Father, and it sufficeth us" (John 14:8).

You have to think a moment about how to pronounce "sufficeth." (There's no trick. It's "suffice-eth.")

"Seething sea" adds another problem word ("ceaseth") and incorporates alliteration. It was by far the hardest tongue twister, and was in fact ten times harder than even the notably difficult "sixth sick sheik." Only 3 percent of attempts were judged correct. Everyone who tried it lisped "ceaseth" into "ceatheth" and "sufficeth" into "suffitheth." You can listen to other people muff it, practice it in your head, and it still comes out like it would be pronounced by Sylvester of Looney Tunes fame. You can say the sentence very, very slowly, but saying it with a natural rhythm is difficult.

The raw success rate may be misleading. It is clearly more difficult to say a long phrase than a short one, all things being equal. To remedy this, the table also gives the success rate on a per-word basis (the $n$th root of the raw success rate, where $n$ is the number of words in the tongue twister). This made a few changes in the rankings. The long "Peter Piper," third most difficult in total success rate, fell to near the bottom of the list. "Toy boat" fell behind "Chicks." "Seething sea" is still the hardest.

There is no reason to believe that the English language

has the most difficult tongue twisters. You know those clicks in the language of the African Bushmen? Well, they've got tongue twisters based on them. *(Iqaqa laziqikaqika kwaze kwaqhawaka uqhoqhoqha* requires three !s in the last word. It means: "The skunk rolled down and ruptured its larynx.")

Tone languages (where variations of pitch distinguish words) allow subtle forms of unpronounceability. Native American and African languages have many so-called tone twisters. The following Yoruba (Nigeria) phrase is both a regular tongue twister and a tone twister:

*Òpòlopò opoló kò mo pé òpòlopò òpòlò lopolo lopolopo,*

which loosely translates:

*Many frogs do not know that most frogs have brains.*

So difficult are these tone-language tongue twisters that at least one was used during the Nigerian civil war to identify spies who were not native speakers of the regional dialect. That tongue twister goes:

*Mo ra dòdò ní Ìddó;*
*Mo jè dòdò ní Ìddó;*
*Mo fi owo dòdò r' omò ònídòdò níidodo nìÌddó.*

which means,

*I bought fried plantains at Iddo;*
*I ate fried plantains at Iddo;*

*I wiped my hands on the navel of the fried-plantain seller at Iddo.*

Those who failed to say the tongue twister correctly were detained or imprisoned. One is inclined to accept the view of linguists who say these tone twisters are harder than any English tongue twisters.

# THE
# SCARIEST
# AMUSEMENT
# PARK RIDE

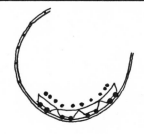

# RAMPANT BRAGGADOCIO

is the norm in the amusement park business. The Beast at Kings Island, near Cincinnati, is "the ultimate dream of every coaster designer and every park in the country," according to William C. Price, who is general manager of the park. "There can't be another one like it!" But *uncannily like it* is the "#1 roller coaster in the entire country," the Riverside Cyclone at Riverside Park, Agawam, Mass. The Riverside Cyclone is styled "not only the most vicious roller coaster ever, but . . . also the most unique." The equally unique Texas Cyclone at Houston's AstroWorld bills itself as the No. 1 roller coaster in the world. At that, amusement parks are in the midst of a building frenzy that promises to trash all existing superlatives. In 1988, Great America in Gurnee, Ill., opened the Shock Wave, described as "the BIG one . . . the tallest and fastest super steel roller coaster in the world." The spring of 1989 demolished two records. In April, Six Flags Great Adventure park of Jackson,

N.J., opened what it said was the highest and fastest coaster in the world: the Great American Scream Machine. Three weeks later, Cedar Point park in Sandusky, Ohio, opened the Magnum XL-200, saying *it* was the highest and fastest. In 1990 Magic Mountain in Valencia, Calif., unveiled what its president called "the most frightening ride on earth," the Viper.

Despite promotional overkill, some amusement park rides are bigger, faster, or scarier than others. There is an organization called American Coaster Enthusiasts whose members periodically vote for the best new roller coaster. One year it was the Riverside Cyclone, which is the basis of that park's claim of preeminence. Such outside testimonials are at a premium. Whenever a newspaper runs a feature with somebody's top-ten list of rides, the named parks cite it for years in their brochures and press releases, long after it could have much relevance. The Coney Island Cyclone's press release quotes a decade-old issue of *Town and Country*—practically the journal of coasterology—that rates it "by far the perfect roller coaster." In recent years, the ride most often mentioned as best or scariest or most thrilling by bona fide disinterested parties is probably the Texas Cyclone. In *Smithsonian* magazine, Robert Cartmell, an art professor at the State University of New York at Albany and well-known connoisseur of roller coasters, called the Texas Cyclone "the greatest thrill ride built since the golden age of coasters in the 1920s." It was also rated No. 1 in a 1984 article in *People* magazine. On the other hand, the Texas Cyclone did not even make a top-ten coaster list published in *Money* magazine in 1989.

Some people like restful, scenic rides. Others don't. It ought to be possible to identify the most thrilling ride, though. That is primarily a matter of dimensions and engineering, of height and speed and acceleration. The only specific way parks rate rides for fear is the height requirement. That helps identify the monster rides at any park, but it is too vague to do much more. Repeat customers is a better measure. At most rides, you stand in line and see the people getting off the ride leave. The proportion of exiting passengers who swear *never, ever,* to go on the ride again ought to tell you something about how scary a ride is.

There are many types of frightening, or at least disorienting, rides other than roller coasters. No haunted house attraction would be scary to the average twelve-year-old. Somewhat in the same line but more expensively produced is Universal Studio Tours' "Earthquake—The Big One"—the only ride based on a real catastrophe, the 1906 San Francisco earthquake that killed 503. At its opening, "the world's first re-creation of a monster 8.3 quake" had some psychologists warning people not to take their young and trauma-prone children. When the 1989 quake hit San Francisco, management closed down the ride for two days out of respect for reality.

Don't expect period sets of old Frisco. The only connection to San Francisco is the magnitude of the simulated quake. The tram takes you into a simulated subway tunnel. (The ride has drawn snipes from humorless people at both San Francisco's BART and Los Angeles's Metro Rail, insisting that in a real earthquake a subway station would be one of the safest places to be.) At the first pre-shock, the tour guide says, "Nothing to be worried about, folks. Just one of the hundred or so little shakes we have in the city each year." Heh-heh. Then the tram rocks back and forth while fabricated calamities erupt. The roof caves in (involving an ersatz "11,000-pound slab of concrete"). Of all the bum luck—the collapse sends a propane tanker veering toward the tram. It hits a severed electrical main shooting purple sparks and explodes into a ball of flame. A "Bay Transit" subway car rams into the truck and rips apart. Finally, an unexplained flood surges down the subway entrance and barely wets your feet in the open-air tram. It's one of several near-identical floods you see on the Universal tour.

Larry Lester, Universal's technical affairs director, told the *Los Angeles Times* that the ride simulates the "seven basic terrors": "fear of an unstable earth, of electrocution, being buried alive, fire, darkness, abandonment and drowning." But don't leave Grandma at home: "This is not going to be something that details people being horrifically injured," another Universal spokesman assured. Lester claimed that the ride would be "one of the safest places to be in a real event"—forgetting that the Los Angeles subway would be *the* safest place.

But it's not very scary. The shaking is mild compared with a big roller coaster or other rides. Besides, you're in the same tram car you take throughout the two-hour tour. You basically know they're not going to scrap it. The roof caving in and the truck sliding toward you are in shaky slow motion and too neat to be real. If you could blindfold some out-of-town visitors, put them on the ride, take the blindfolds off, and tell them this is the Los Angeles subway, maybe *then* all this stuff would work. Otherwise, it's not frightening, and not even quite as memorable as the King Kong deal.

The perils on a roller coaster seem more real. The roller coaster has evolved over decades, producing many subspecies. One of the few living fossils from the so-called golden age of coasters is the Coney Island Cyclone. Just the name "Cyclone" is a big deal to coaster buffs. Applied to dozens of coasters across the country, it evokes the Harry Guy Traver designs of the 1920s. The Coney Island model is the only surviving Traver Cyclone.

There is possibly more rational fear here than with the contemporary rides. The superstructure is creaky old wood rather than silently efficient steel. The adjacent amusement necropolis—ruins of another coaster and the old parachute jump—add to the ambiance of structural neglect. Like most full-strength coasters, the Cyclone has signs warning off the weak and infirm. "Exceptionally large persons," as they tactfully put it, are placed on notice, as are the usual high-risk groups of heart patients and expectant mothers. Ditto for those with "recent surgery." A cartoonish picture shows a guy's stitches coming open and vital organs tumbling out. And: "Hold on to your wigs."

The track is extraordinarily steep on the first drop. Slope is deceptive, at least while you're riding the thing. Go on any big coaster and you'll swear that you were plunging almost straight down. Once you get off, you can see that the dip's angle to the ground was only about 45 degrees. The Coney Island Cyclone appears to hold a record with a claimed maximum angle of 58.7 degrees. The Cyclone is scary enough to hold its own with many of the more contemporary rides. You keep thinking you'll hit your head on the top of tunnels through the framework. The Cyclone is not especially high by contemporary standards, though.

A bigger, better version of the Coney Island coaster is Houston's Texas Cyclone. Of 1975 vintage, the Texas Cyclone was designed by noted coaster architect William Cobb after Traver's original. (Cobb, incidentally, is a Beethoven-like figure who has never ridden some of his coasters because of his heart surgery.) Cobb jazzed up the Coney Island design with bigger plunges and tighter curves. The height of drop is 93 feet compared with 85 for Coney Island. Strangely, the Texas Cyclone is less steep, the maximum inclination being only 53 degrees. Despite its billing as the No. 1 coaster, the Texas Cyclone is neither the highest, the steepest, nor the fastest coaster. All in all, the effect is very comparable to the Coney Island model—perhaps a little smoother; little if any scarier.

Hard-core coaster fans are often picky about seats. Oddly, the Texas Cyclone requires that you be 60 inches tall to ride in the back seat (48 inches is the height requirement for the other seats). The frontmost and backmost seats are said to be the best, front for the view and back for whiplash effects. The latter effect is questionable. The back seat doesn't go anywhere the other seats don't.

Larger yet is Cedar Point's Magnum XL-200, the tallest American coaster at this writing. Other than height, its main distinction is three tunnels jazzed up with strobe lights and allegedly nontoxic smoke. The Magnum is just over 200 feet high.

Most of the biggest coasters are in the Sunbelt, where a year-round operating season can finance their massive construction and overhead costs. The most popular year-round coaster is Space Mountain, existing in cookie-cutter duplicates at Orlando's Disney World and Anaheim, Calif.'s Disneyland. Although among the tamest of "adult" roller coasters, the two Space Mountains are the scariest rides at the Disney parks. They have a chicken exit for those who reconsider in mid-queue, and you see an occasional kid or grandparent freak out.

Each Space Mountain is about 175 feet high. Technically that made them the tallest coasters in the country prior to the opening of the Magnum XL-200. The 175 feet is measured from the ground to the purely decorative needle on top. The coaster stays inside the fake mountain, and it never plunges more than a fraction of the total height. The actual maximum speed, claims the park with commendable frankness, is 28 miles per hour.

The two remarkable things about Space Mountain are the special effects and the fact that it's indoors and in the dark. The "stars" projected on the ceiling move backward relative to the coaster. This creates a painless illusion of speed. The "meteors" look like—and supposedly are—movies of chocolate-chip cookies.

In our informal sample, several exiting passengers said they'd never go on it again. But Disney World isn't much of a thrill-ride park, and probably many of its visitors had never been on an adult-oriented coaster. Space Mountain is *much* less gut-wrenching than the Coney Island or Texas Cyclone.

Many coaster enthusiasts dismiss all of the above. The salient distinction of most contemporary thrill rides is a complete 360-degree loop. The loop-the-loop is not new. Late-nineteenth-century Coney Island had a "Flip-Flap Coaster," a true loop-the-loop in which cars did a full 360-degree somersault. This was reportedly murder on people's necks and probably would have been a legalistic bonanza in today's litigious society. Later designs used an elliptical loop believed to be less neck-wrenching, but it too fizzled commercially after the novelty wore off. The public liked the idea; it was just too uncomfortable. For many years, no one built loop-the-loops.

The modern age of looping coasters began in the 1970s with the construction of the Revolution at Magic Mountain near Los Angeles. The Revolution's all-steel loop is in the shape of an inverted teardrop. This shape increases centrifugal force just at the peak when it is needed to keep riders in their seats. That allows a lower overall speed for a loop-the-loop, creating a more comfortable ride. This loop and the greater strength of the steel-tubing track are the basis of contemporary gravity-defying rides.

By anyone's standards, the Revolution is scarier than a plain coaster that doesn't loop. It's a brave rider indeed who can keep his eyes open the first time.

Just like the plain-vanilla coasters, the looping rides have been progressively amplified. Magic Mountain upped its own ante with Shock Wave, a loop-the-loop coaster where you're standing up. They want you to think that makes it worse, but it's really about the same. Strapping yourself in is complicated enough to require a diagram showing how to do it. You raise a "seat," which is basically a rubber fist, into your crotch, put one arm through a harness, pull down a safety bar, and you're ready for fun. The effect is genuinely unnerving, but you find that pressing your feet down onto the floor has a tranquilizing effect. Two apparently unintentional touches: Coins from people's pockets litter a green mesh above you as you stand in line, and real birds of prey circle the ride.

Magic Mountain is owned by the Six Flags company, which has parks nationwide. Many of the rides at Six Flags' parks are standardized and can be found at the other parks. However, the names are inconsistent. The Shock Wave at Great America in Gurnee, north of Chicago, is different. This Shock Wave is a regular sit-down ride and is billed as the world's biggest roller coaster.

The Illinois Shock Wave has *seven* loops: three regular ones, two "corkscrew" loops (following the threads of an imaginary horizontal screw), and two paired "boomerang" loops that quickly reverse direction. No signs warn pregnant women or heart patients. The more believable hazard here is "ear jewelry & hearing aids," apt to become lost or deadly projectiles.

The first indication you have that this ride is something different is the queue of exiting riders. As a rule, no matter how much people may have hated it, they come off a roller coaster smiling. Here they weren't making the pretense. Most passengers were holding their necks (you are told to keep your head against the headrest) and not smiling.

The most uniquely memorable part of the Great America Shock Wave is the ascent. It takes an incredibly long time for the train to climb up to the crest of the first hill (about a minute, but it seems longer). You get higher and higher, look down at the tiny cars in the parking lot, and still you ascend. Then comes the first drop. It is steep and banked heavily. Even from the ground, it looks like the train has tumbled off the track.

It takes more presence of mind than you've probably got to identify which of the three types of loops you're on at the time.

You'll just remember going upside down again and again and again.

The Houston AstroWorld's Greezed Lightnin' and the near-identical Montezooma's Revenge at Knott's Berry Farm in Buena Park, Calif., are an unusual variation on the loop-the-loop. Each has a track that is a loop with two free ends of track projecting up and out into space. The cars are accelerated from rest by a special drive. They go through the loop, then shoot up one end of track. The cars don't quite have enough momentum to make it to the top. Rather, the cars reverse, go through the loop backward (at exasperatingly slow speed), and then up another incline of track.

What makes a roller coaster scary? The stoic might object that no ride is bad as long as you get off it safely. The annual roller-coaster death toll in the United States is about 1.5 a year. That's less than lightning or tornadoes (each kills about 100 people a year in the United States alone); more than running with the bulls in Pamplona (just 14 deaths in this century). Many deaths are on rickety old relics. Of the big, well-known rides, the Colossus at Magic Mountain and the Beast at Cincinnati's Kings Island have each claimed a life. In each case it was apparently the victim's fault.

Speed is part of what makes a ride thrilling. "I recently read of a roller coaster that went 100 mph. Is this possible? I say no. My husband says yes. Find out, please," asked a 1987 letter to Ann Landers. Ann responded that a 100-mph coaster was impossible because "the fastest roller coaster in the world is in

Gurnee, Ill. It goes 66.31 mph. Many promoters exaggerate for commercial reasons."

Ann was right on the mark. *Gross* exaggeration of speed is near-universal. Ann was referring to Six Flags' Great America. We, however, find no special reason to believe Six Flags' claim just because it is given to two decimal places. Employees of the same Six Flags organization claim a speed of 85 m.p.h. for its Colossus roller coaster near Los Angeles, and this is a wild exaggeration.

Speed is open to overstatement because there's no way for riders to measure it. A claimed speed is often just a generous estimate based on the height of drop. Tell the public they're going a hundred miles an hour: What are they going to do, sue the park?

A roller coaster is a simple machine. There is no motor, no accelerator pedal. A lift drags the cars up that first hill, then gravity does all the rest. The top speed of a roller coaster can be estimated from the maximum height.

The *free-fall speed* is how hard an object dropped from rest at a given height hits the pavement. Neglecting air resistance, it depends only on the height of drop. For a height of 100 feet, it's 54.7 miles an hour. That's how fast a bowling ball, a person, or a roller-coaster car dropped from 100 feet would be going when it hit the ground.

A roller coaster without a motor cannot exceed this free-fall speed. Given the maximum height of the track, it is a simple matter to figure the free-fall speed. The height must be measured from the track's highest point to its lowest point. A coaster that is 100 feet above the ground at its highest and 10 feet above at its lowest has an effective height of 90 feet.

It is unlikely that a coaster would attain its theoretical maximum speed. The cars are constrained by the track to move in a less than sheer drop, and there is considerable friction with the track no matter how well greased it may be. If brakes are used, the speed is all the less. Brakes are a sore point with purists. Designers include them to reduce maintenance costs. The faster the cars go, the more strain they place on the coaster superstructure, and the more frequently it must be inspected, repaired, or replaced altogether.

The 1984 article in *People* magazine claimed that the Beast at Kings Island hits 70 miles an hour on the first trip of the morning, when it is run without brakes. This would appear to be physically impossible. Kings Island reports that the Beast is 105 feet high at its peak. The lowest point of track is in a gully cut 36 feet into the ground. That makes the total drop 141 feet. If you took the Beast's train of cars and dropped them vertically from 141 feet, they would attain a maximum speed of only 65 miles an hour. The fact that the brakes are off can't better this speed; this is what would occur in the complete absence of friction.

The fact is, the drive to the amusement park is usually faster than the roller coaster. The difference is that cars are engineered to negate the sensation of motion and roller coasters to play it up. A typical "adult" coaster has a maximum speed of about 38 miles per hour. On tight curves, it is rarely more than 25 mph. The Beast, one of the fastest coasters in existence, barely attains highway speeds.

Cedar Point's Magnum XL-200, the tallest U.S. coaster at this writing, has a 201-foot hill. The trough of the first drop is just under 10 feet high, so the total drop is about 191 feet. That drop would allow a theoretical speed of 76 mph. The park says the Magnum tops out at 72 mph.

The table shows ten of the tallest and probably fastest coasters in North America. Actually, the tallest coasters in operation are in Japan. Japan's monster Moonsault Scramble at Fujikyu Highland Park on the slopes of Mount Fuji is 246 feet high. Even if all of that were a sheer drop, the maximum possible speed would be 86 miles per hour. The park claims a believable top speed of 65.2 mph.

| Ride | Park | Location | Height | Maximum Drop | Claimed Speed | Free-Fall Speed* |
|------|------|----------|--------|--------------|---------------|------------------|
| Magnum XL-200 | Cedar Point | Sandusky, Ohio | 201 | 191 | 72 | 76 |
| Viper | Magic Mountain | Valencia, Calif. | 188 | 188 | 70 | 75 |
| Great American Scream Machine | Great Adventure | Jackson, N.J. | 173 | 173 | 68 | 72 |
| Shock Wave | Great America | Gurnee, Ill. | 170 | 155 | 65 | 68 |
| American Eagle | Great America | Gurnee, Ill. | 127 | 147.4 | 66.32 | 66 |

| Ride | Park | Location | Height | Maximum Drop | Claimed Speed | Free-Fall Speed* |
|------|------|----------|--------|--------------|---------------|-------------------|
| Mindbender | Canada Fantasyland | Edmonton, Alta. | 145 | 145 | 55 | 66 |
| Tidal Wave | Great America | Santa Clara, Calif. | 142.5 | 142.5 | 55 | 65 |
| Beast | Kings Island | Cincinnati | 105 | 141 | 72 | 65 |
| Vortex | Kings Island | Cincinnati | 148 | 138 | .50 | 64 |
| Gemini | Cedar Point | Sandusky, Ohio | 125.33 | 118 | 60 | 59 |
| Colossus | Magic Mountain | Valencia, Calif. | 125 | 115 | 85 | 59 |

* $\sqrt{2gh}$, where $h$ is the initial height and $g$ is the gravitational acceleration, 32 feet per second squared. Results (in feet per second) are multiplied by 0.6818 to convert to miles per hour.

---

Speed isn't everything. Perfectly smooth rides at 10 mph and 100 mph feel the same, except for the air rushing by. Moving at high speed in a horizontal direction is no big deal. It's too much like riding in a car.

What you actually feel in your gut is acceleration, changes in velocity. Acceleration presses you into your seat, causes motion sickness, and generally creates the sensation of motion. A park can build a higher, faster coaster, but it can't much increase the actual forces on the passenger. Designers have to keep the g forces within human tolerances—and, indeed, comfort levels.

Big looping rides like the Great American Scream Machine and Great America's Shock Wave demonstrate the diminishing returns of scaling up. Shock Wave's claimed maximum g force, which occurs at the bottom of the first drop, is 3.5 g's. That's not much more than in considerably smaller coasters. (A good fighter pilot can take about 10 g's before blacking out.) The force at the top of Shock Wave's teardrop loops is 1.5 g's up, partially neutralized by 1 g of gravity for a net upward force of half a g. One-half negative g is essentially standard with all contemporary teardrop loops. Consequently, the actual experience of riding Shock Wave is not that much different from riding any of the big steel looping coasters. You're tugged in the harness a little more, and the extra height jabs at any acrophobia. That's about it.

Judging by screams, *falling* is the scary part of any roller coaster. Possibly the claim of some psychologists that the two primal fears are of falling and of loud noises applies here. When a coaster is going up a hill, you hear a few nervous titters. The screams come when the coaster plunges downward. The steeper the plunge, the louder the screams. Surprisingly, the correlation between downward motion and screams applies even to the complex loop-the-loops. The loudest screams (and, subjectively, the scariest moments) come in the initial plunge, not on entering a loop.

The main physical sensation associated with falling is weightlessness. That in itself isn't always bad. Weightlessness is actually kind of fun when you're moving upward. Then it's like the momentary euphoria when a car hits a bump in the road. The corresponding effect on a roller coaster, when a fast-moving car just tops a hill, isn't bad either. The sick sensation apparently requires that you be moving downward while weightless. The scariest ride, therefore, should be the one where you fall the greatest distance, unrestrained, at the sheerest angle.

There are several rides that create the sensation of falling more or less directly. One is the parachute jump, originally built at Coney Island for the 1939–40 World's Fair and long since razed. Bigger versions have been built in recent years at Dallas's Six Flags Over Texas and Knott's Berry Farm of Buena Park, Calif. In a parachute jump, you ride to the top of a tower in an open-air elevator and glide down attached to a parachute guided by cables. The contemporary models are about 200 feet high, with an actual drop of 165 feet. That's more than even the Illinois Shock Wave roller coaster, and it's a vertical drop.

The brightly colored "parachutes" are strictly for show. They're honeycombed with holes and wouldn't do much good if the cables snapped. Two or three people get in a gondola that is essentially a metal cage connected to cables. The cables run up to the top of a tower that often doubles as the support for one of those rotating observation decks. The elevator mechanism pulls the gondola quickly up. The ascent isn't bad at all. At the top you're usually at the highest point in the park.

Then you fall. After the initial sinking feeling, it's fun. The parachute billows out but doesn't really do anything. Brakes slow the gondola down as it nears the ground.

Some people are acutely discomfited by tram rides or by

space-needle-type observation decks. A parachute jump is just as bad. The gondola affords an unrestricted view straight down. It is also worse because the fear of falling is realized.

But for most people parachute jumps aren't that bad. Hardly anyone screams, maybe because there's no crowd. The ride dilutes the sensation of falling. Speed and acceleration are less than in a real fall or in a plunging roller coaster. The actual speed at Knott's Berry Farm's Parachute Sky Jump is claimed to be a leisurely 18 miles per hour. The ride takes about ten seconds, which gives you a chance to accommodate to the experience of slow-motion falling. Many people who went on it went right back in line to do it again.

Another type of ride does not have a generic name but is typified by Magic Mountain's Z-Force. A giant 50-passenger swing shaped like a fighter jet or a ship sways back and forth, the arc increasing each time. Soon it makes an almost complete turn. You hang suspended upside down, held in place only by the harness. Then you fall back down again. The swings are a piece of cake; it's the stalled moments that make this ride what it is. Actually rather terrifying, it doesn't look half bad from the line. The park claims that riders are suspended nearly 100 feet high at the top of the arc and states a maximum force of 3 g's.

Worse yet is another widespread type of ride, the free fall. Magic Mountain's FreeFall is billed as "the ultimate white-knuckle adventure!" It is virtually a parachute jump without parachutes. Four at a time, you ride a glass-enclosed gondola up to the top of a tower. You have a magnificent view of the Santa Clarita Valley. The gondola lingers there a few seconds, long enough to let you realize that this isn't a "ride" in the usual sense, that you're just going to fall 90 feet straight down. If there were a panic button you could push to chicken out, it would get a lot of use. The gondola jerks forward a few feet, and then—WHAM!—like Wile E. Coyote, you plummet downward.

The elevator is on a track that starts out vertical. You really do fall straight down and essentially unrestrained. Toward the bottom, the track curves off to the horizontal. The gondola ends up horizontal, passengers on their backs.

Magic Mountain quotes a top speed of 55 mph, which is probably only a trifle exaggerated. The 131-foot-tall tower has a total drop of 98.4 feet. About 60 feet of that is vertical. The physical free-fall speed for a 98.4-foot drop is 54.2 mph. FreeFall ought to approach that theoretical maximum closer than roller coasters in view of the modest friction in the early part of the fall. A computerized mechanism determines the weight of the loaded gondola and applies braking force as needed. The system is "aware" of the position of the falling gondola via sensors in the track. The ride proper takes a mere 2.5 seconds—giving this the greatest ratio of wait-in-line time to ride time of any ride in operation (about 45 minutes on a weekend: 2.5 seconds, or 1,080:1).

FreeFall's exiting passengers seemed to be the most convinced that they had made a horrible mistake in getting on it. That's particularly impressive in view of Magic Mountain's customer profile. As the only Six Flags park to compete directly against a Disney park, it writes off the family trade and focuses on hell-for-leather rides for adolescents. Guards regularly frisk suspected gang members for Uzis at the entrance gate. There are five roller coasters, the tamest of which is rougher than anything at Disneyland.

There is no worst free-fall ride because they are all virtually identical. Each has a drop of just under 100 feet. They're built by a Swiss firm, Intamin A.G., the Rolls-Royce of serious rides. Intamin also made the Parachute Sky Jump, Montezooma's Revenge, and similar rides. Most of the Six Flags parks have an Intamin free fall. It goes by the name of FreeFall not only at Magic Mountain but at Great Adventure in Jackson, N.J. The ride is called Skyscreamer in Houston (Astroland), Texas Cliffhanger in Dallas (Six Flags Over Texas), and the Edge in Santa Clara, Calif. (Great America).

Our subjective impressions confirm the exit poll. Free-fall rides are the most unnerving currently in operation. Fear is instantaneous, so the free-fall ride packs all it has into that two-second drop. The worst moment of a big roller coaster is the initial plunge. FreeFall is a more intense version of that worst moment. You fall vertically downward under full force of gravity a greater distance than in any roller coaster or other ride.

# THE MOST DELICIOUS GOURMET FOOD

# "MY LAST MEAL ON EARTH"

has long been a popular essay topic among gourmets and bon vivants. Nothing short of impending death, the conceit goes, suffices to strip away the usual foodie pretensions. Patent fads like edible flowers, radicchio, or miniature vegetables must pall in the hour of doom. So must mere exotica, hoary "gourmet items" like pickled quail's eggs or chocolate-covered ants. It's your last meal; if you could have *anything,* what would it be? It amounts to the ultimate riddle of gastronomy, the question that is as profound as any question about food is going to be. What is the best-tasting food of all?

In *Down the Kitchen Sink* (1974), Beverley Nichols asserts that terrapin is "the most delicious thing I have ever tasted." According to Nichols, "George Gershwin, leaning towards me and speaking *à haute voix,* informed me that it cost twenty dollars a portion, which I can well believe. . . . I had never had it before, have never had it since, and doubt whether I shall ever have it again." That's all very well and interesting until you read someone else's opinion of terrapin and they say it tastes just like chicken, only a little on the bland side. Uh-huh.

Sir Francis Colchester-Wemyss thought bêche-de-mer soup was the best thing on earth—no, make that "what the angels get when they order turtle soup on special feast days in paradise," as he put it. A bêche-de-mer is a sea cucumber, a sluglike creature related to the starfish, that is popular in China.

These are but two of hundreds of mutually incompatible claims to the effect that a certain gratuitously obscure food is *the most delicious thing on earth*. There are two problems with them. First, they're one person's opinion. You never know if the writer just has eccentric tastes. Second, you don't always know what else the writer has tasted. The very experts who are pronouncing one food the best may not have tasted other widely esteemed foods—particularly those outside their own culinary traditions—or may have at best a hazy memory of them. The element of one-on-one comparison is missing.

To remedy that, we arranged a blind tasting of several rare or exotic foods. We were interested mainly in foods rare enough not to be found in the average American supermarket but which have been praised over and over again as not just very good but as the best thing an expert gourmet had ever tasted. A panel of volunteer tasters compared these foods all at once and ranked them by preference. Their aggregate evaluation should give you an idea of how likely it is that you would share the critics' opinions.

A few "last meals" have actually been prepared and eaten. The nineteenth-century British chef Alexis Soyer served a celebrated "most recherché" meal at the Reform Club, London, on May 9, 1846. In recent decades, the closest thing to a real-life last meal was the famous $4,000 dinner Craig Claiborne and Pierre Franey ate at Paris's Chez Denis restaurant in 1975. It is interesting as a snapshot of what two of the most respected contemporary food critics thought was really good, damn the cost.

They didn't have to worry about cost because the meal ran Claiborne only $300. American Express had donated a dinner for two to a public television fund-raising auction. The dinner could take place at any restaurant in the world—provided that it accepted the American Express card—and there was no limit on expense. Well, you can't much blame Claiborne for taking advantage of that. Claiborne's $300 bid was highest. After deliberation he and *New York Times* colleague Franey selected Chez Denis for the dinner.

Chez Denis's owner originally told Claiborne that their best meal would cost $2,000 or $3,000. But suppose money was no object, Claiborne countered. The owner reconsidered and said $4,000—for a traditional dinner with nine wines for four people. Claiborne insisted that it had to be for just two people; that was the deal. The restaurateur replied that the price would still be $4,000 because the nine wine bottles would be opened and many recipes could not be scaled down.

Description of the dinner made the front page of the *New York Times,* and drew an almost unanimously outraged reaction from readers. Many pointed out that the $4,000 could have fed thousands of hungry people. Some took issue with

Claiborne's curmudgeonly review (he complained that the food was served on "ordinary" plates). "I enjoyed the $4,000 front-page Parisian dinner spread so much that I had to clear my palate with ices and sherbets between paragraphs," wrote Mary-Lou Weisman of Westport, Conn., to the editors.

The meal consisted of 31 dishes. Claiborne and Franey could do no more than sample the boggling variety set before them. Courses included beluga caviar, chartreuse of partridge, ortolans en brochette, foie gras in aspic, woodcock breasts, cold pheasant with hazelnuts, fillets of wild duck en salmis, veal in pastry with truffles, and fruit ices. Wines accounted for at least half the meal's stupendous cost. Claiborne rated a 1918 Château Latour as "perhaps the best Bordeaux we had ever known." It sold for about $100 a bottle in New York, reported the *Times,* but the restaurant had to open three bottles to get one in drinkable condition. The most expensive wine was a 1929 Romanée-Conti, which cost about $500 a bottle retail.

Let's start, as Claiborne and Franey did, with caviar, the most accessible of the foods we'll be discussing here. Everyone's had caviar. It was that black stuff in pastry shells, and it tasted fishy. Most of us would have no trouble accepting caviar as one of life's little disappointments were it not for the self-appointed experts who shake their heads and insist that *that* wasn't caviar. It is accepted as an article of faith that real, fresh caviar isn't fishy or salty and tastes so good you'd go nuts if you ever came close to it.

"Caviar" is not a regulated term like "Bordeaux." You can call any fish eggs caviar. About 15,000 pounds of stuff labeled "caviar" is consumed annually. Fish is perishable, and so are eggs. It is no surprise that fish eggs are perishable. To produce a caviar that keeps without refrigeration, it must be denatured with heat and salt. In the late 1800s, Americans learned how to do this using roe of native fish of the Hudson River valley, the Pacific Northwest, and elsewhere. Salmon ("red caviar"), whitefish, lumpfish, tuna, and mullet are the commonest species. This lesser caviar is what you see sitting unrefrigerated in a strange Lucite safe at the front of a supermarket. It is pasteurized and heavily salted, resulting in a shelf life that holds its own with Vienna sausages and Spam. The argument, repeated in one gourmet treatise after another, is that judging what fresh caviar is like from this processed product is like judging fish from a tin of anchovies. Pasteurized caviar is not exactly cheap ($3 an ounce or so). It is much cheaper than fresh caviar.

"Real" caviar comes from Russia or Iran (at this writing, the United States has an embargo on the Iranian product). This caviar is the roe of sturgeon of the Caspian Sea and its tributary rivers. Producing caviar isn't like running down to the hen house for a few eggs. The sturgeon are clubbed to death on the spot and slit open to get the roe. Only their nightmarish appearance prevents this from being a fur-seal-like cause célèbre. Since the roe must be processed within about two hours of the catch, the processing stations are built on artificial wooden islands in shoals of the Caspian or near the mouths of rivers. Limited supply and the inevitable losses of a perishable product keep prices high.

The various grades of caviar come from different species. In descending order of roe size, they are beluga, osetra, sevruga, sterlyad, and sterlet. The beluga can live up to three centuries, grow 24 feet long, and weigh well over a ton. The biggest beluga roe is the size of peas. Part of the caviar experience is the feel of bursting the grains against the roof of the mouth. Usually beluga is preferred for this. Beluga is also the most plentiful type. The fish, being bigger, produces more roe—as many as 3 million eggs.

Caviar is at its best for a few days after processing. It is said to have no fishy taste whatsoever. Then it declines slowly even if it is kept properly refrigerated. Experts say caviar spoils if stored at temperatures above 40 degrees F. Once a can is opened, it deteriorates more quickly. Don't even think about what happens if it's frozen. The upshot is that caviar has to travel a long distance in a short time with no more than a few degrees' variation in temperature. The fishy taste, with caviar as with other seafood, is a sign of impending spoilage. Boric acid, added to caviar that will be sold in Europe, prevents fishiness and lends a slight tartness. The United States considers boric acid too toxic for food. Our caviar (even the imported) doesn't have it.

Knowing caviar eaters are finicky about freshness. In *La Bonne Table* (1964), hotelier Ludwig Bemelmans tells of a Parisian gourmand who had Cartier design a gold ball for the end of his watch chain. In restaurants he dropped the ball from the height of one foot into a plateful of caviar. If it passed through the roe to the plate, it was good. If the ball got stuck, he returned the caviar. This may sound like the height of aristocratic affectation, but Cartier later mass-produced such a gold ball for testing caviar.

You get a range of opinions on which grade of caviar is the best. Sterlyad caviar was once favored at the courts of the czars and the emperors of Austria. Many Europeans still favor the smaller-grained types, and some argue that large-grained beluga does not travel as well as other kinds. Golden caviar was reserved for the czars, Stalin, the Shah of Iran, and their cronies. Actually, most agree that color does not make much difference in terms of taste. Colors range from black through gray almost to white, and golden through greenish brown. Golden caviar is usually a greenish color. Caviar taken near spawning time is gray.

American experts usually say that the kind of caviar to get is light gray or golden beluga malassol. "Malassol" means packed with a minimum (about 4 percent) of salt. Since salt tends to cover defects, malassol is the equivalent of brut champagne. A *nastavnic* is the expert who tastes the caviar and determines how much salt to add. Connoisseurs claim to recognize the *nastavnic* by the flavor of the finished product. Fresh beluga malassols sell for about $30 an ounce retail; maybe $60 an ounce for a supplier's premium variety.

A *New York Times* article on caviar rated as best the "Imperial" beluga sold by Caviarteria, a New York dealer. Our comparison used Caviarteria's "Imperial" golden malassol beluga.

Idolatry of truffles has exceeded even that of caviar. Though prized since classical times, truffles came into their own in the early nineteenth century. France just about went ape over them. "Truffles became so scarce that they were escorted through the city with armed guards, and men ruined themselves in order to prove their social stability by serving one stuffed turkey," wrote M. F. K. Fisher.

Truffles are de rigueur for last meals. Claiborne and Franey had them with veal in pastry; César Ritz served *truffes en papillotes* to ten prominent financiers at the notorious money's-no-object blowout of his day. Alexis Soyer wanted to include orlotan-stuffed truffles (rather than the other way around) in his most recherché meal. Ortolans are little birds, so it would have taken very large truffles or very small ortolans. The ortolans didn't arrive in time for the meal, though.

"The truffle is the diamond of the art of cookery," contends the godfather of gourmands, Jean Anthelme Brillat-Savarin, in *The Physiology of Taste* (1825). He mentions truffle-stuffed turkeys as a test of the serious eater. Thackeray gets all worked up about them in *Memories of Gourmandizing:* "Presently, we were aware of an odour coming towards us, something musky, fiery, savoury, mysterious,—a hot drowsy smell, that lulls the senses, and yet enflames them—the *truffles* were coming." And Colette swooned, "If I can't have too many truffles, I'll do without truffles."

Like caviar, truffles are deceptively familiar. They're the black things, practically flyspecks, in pâtés. Actually, you're lucky to get visible specks. Sometimes it's just pâté with truffle juice. Like holy water, the truffle's very presence confers a culinary blessing, however infinitely diluted. Fine chefs boast of using rice or eggs that have merely been stored overnight with truffles. It's enough to make you think truffles are some kind of hoax. Rest assured that people have eaten enough of a truffle to tell what it tastes like. During France's trufflemania, people cooked and ate them like potatoes.

The mystique of truffles owes a lot to the uncertain supply. They are gathered from the wild, not raised on truffle farms. Someone is always coming up with a scheme to cultivate them that sounds promising and then fizzles out. "Useless efforts! Lying promises!" snarled Brillat-Savarin. The situation is scarcely better today despite earnest and technologically sophisticated attempts.

Even as wild foods go, truffles are unique in being invisible. They grow underground in oak woods, not necessarily on oak roots. Hunting them requires an animal with a good sense of smell. Pigs have keen noses but are unruly and must be muzzled lest they scarf the quarry themselves. Pigs have largely been replaced with dogs. There is a school for truffle hounds in Alba, Italy. The dogs are starved for eight to ten days, then they gorge on dog food mixed with a rotten truffle. Hunting truffles is done at night lest competing hunters see where finds are made. Secret maps of truffle grounds are passed down in families. (The romance of truffle hunting has spawned a small literature. In *Serve It Forth,* M. F. K. Fisher repeats the memorable if apocryphal story that elderly virgins were used to hunt truffles. Patricia Highsmith's short story "In the Dead of Truffle Season" concerns a truffle pig who turns on his master, provoked to madness from years of having the morsels snatched from him.)

Truffles are dying out. The English truffle industry vanished completely, the last truffle hunter retiring in 1935. Around the turn of the century, the annual production of truffles worldwide was about 2,000 tons. In 1980 it was 46 tons. In 1985 (a particularly bad year) it was just 15 tons.

This guarantees that truffles remain expensive. The *Guinness Book of World Records* says that "First Choice Black Périgord Truffles" are the most expensive food in the world at

$13.20 for a 0.44 ounce container. They are evidently talking about tinned or bottled truffles, which is misleading because the high markup on tins sold in gourmet stores makes such truffles more expensive than truffles in bulk. Even so, the quoted price is the equivalent of $30 an ounce, and is still cheaper than top-of-the-line caviar. Fresh black truffles (which would be much better than the tinned item anyway) have recently been going for about $800 a kilogram (about $24 an ounce). Italian white truffles have been selling for about $50 an ounce. The Guinness book also mentions that some Arabian truffles sell at SR 5,000 for 3 kilograms. That's about $136 an ounce.

Accounts of the difference in flavor between black and white truffles are unbelievably contradictory. At different times each variety has been preferred. There are subvarieties of each color, so you're never quite sure what kind someone is talking about. The Romans prized Libyan truffles most of all; these were white or reddish. Today the white truffle of gourmets comes from the Piedmont region of Italy. There are also white truffles in North Africa and part of France which differ from the Italian. The white truffle is said to taste of garlic. It is mostly eaten raw. Truffles of various kinds grow in North America but are known mostly to mushroom hobbyists. Colette giddily called the Périgord black truffle "the most capricious, most revered of all those black princesses." The Larousse *Encyclopedia of Cookery* agrees in slightly more restrained language. But *Los Angeles Times* critic Ruth Reichl complained, "I've never understood the mystique that makes otherwise sane people pay obscene sums of money for black lumps that look like coal and taste like smoked tires. . . . This does not, let me hasten to add, in any way reflect upon white truffles, which are, as far as I'm concerned, among the wonders of the world."

Truffles have been suspected both of being an aphrodisiac and of being indigestible. Brillat-Savarin felt compelled to address both issues in *The Physiology of Taste.* He records the breathless confession of an unnamed woman ("What can I say to you, monsieur? I blame the whole thing on the truffles . . ."), then discounts this and concludes that truffles are "not a positive aphrodisiac." On the digestibility question, he says that truffles are "as healthy as they are pleasant, and that if they are eaten in moderation they will be assimilated as smoothly as a letter falls into a mailbox."

As with caviar, there is said to be a world of difference between fresh and canned truffles. The "truffle shavings" restaurants use so skillfully to increase the price of a plate of pasta are usually the canned kind. For our taste test, we wanted to serve fresh truffles whole. For the black truffles, we adapted the recipe Colette gives in *Prisons et Paradis:*

Bathed in a good, very dry white wine—keep the champagne for your banquets, the truffle can do without it—salted without extravagance, peppered with discretion, they can then be cooked in a simple, black, cast-iron stewpot with the lid on. For twenty-five minutes, they must dance in the constant flow of bubbles, drawing with them through the eddies and the foam—like Tritons playing around some darker Amphitrite—a score or so of smallish strips of bacon, fat, but not too fat, which will give body to the stock. No other herbs or spices! And a pestilence upon your rolled napkin, with its taste and odor of lye, last resting place of the cooked truffle! Your truffles must come to the table in their own stock. Do not stint when you serve yourself: the truffle is an appetite creator, an aid to digestion. And as you break open this jewel sprung from a poverty-stricken soil, imagine—if you have never visited it—the desolate kingdom where it rules. For it kills the dog rose, drains life from the oak, and ripens beneath an ungrateful bed of pebbles.

'Umar ibn-Muhammad's *The Perfumed Garden of the Shaykh Nefzawi,* the sixteenth-century Islamic sex manual, describes 36 sexual positions, of which the 24th is considered the best. The missionary position does not even make the list. You feel the same way learning of the praise lavished on foods that most Americans have never even heard of. Ortolan, fugu, cherimoya, mangosteen—their names mean nothing to most Americans, yet people of educated palate have declared them to be the most delectable substances on earth.

Gourmets dote on dozens of species of game birds. Claiborne and Franey's meal at Chez Denis included five types of game (partridge, ortolan, woodcock, pheasant, wild duck) versus just one meat entrée (veal). Opinions on which game bird is best are highly idiosyncratic. Dr. Venner (circa 1620) wrote: "For sweetness and pleasantnesse of taste the Pheasant excelleth all other fowle verily for goodnesse and pleasantnesse of flesh it may of all sylvestriall fowle well challenge the first place at table, for it giveth a most perfect and temperate nourishment to them that be healthy." Sydney Smith agreed: "If there be one pure and elevated pleasure in this world it is a roast pheasant."

Speaking on behalf of grouse, we have Edward Bunyard, who rated it "the king of all birds." André Simon concurred, listing the finest game birds in descending order of delectability as grouse, woodcock, partridge, pheasant, and snipe.

Ortolans are eaten whole, eyeballs and all. That grisly prospectus may not whet American appetites, but ortolans are among the most prized of delicacies in Europe. "Ortolan is, I think, the most wonderful word in the French language, sumptuous in its suggestion and musical in its refrain," wrote Edward Bunyard. "The Romantic authors could not resist their appeal and brought them to the table whenever possible, the most incomparable mouthful that nature has ever produced." Bunyard then confesses that he had never tried them. Even then the birds were extremely hard to come by. Ortolans live in the Old World and eat berries. To prepare them for the table, they are plucked of their feathers and cooked whole. You are supposed to eat everything except the legs.

Brillat-Savarin deemed the figpecker the finest of small birds: "It grows at least as fat as the redbreast or the ortolan, and nature has moreover given it a slight bitterness and a unique flavor so exquisite that they seize upon, flood, and beautify every possible avenue of taste. If a figpecker could grow as big as a pheasant, it would be worth the price of an acre of land." Those already squeamish about ortolans will not agreeably note that Brillat-Savarin contended the figpecker was best raw. "When sportsmen in the Dauphiné hunt in September, they too are armed with salt and with pepper. If one of them happens to bag a plump, perfect figpecker he plucks it, seasons it, carries it for a time in the crown of his hat, and eats it. Such gourmands insist that this is much more delicious than the bird when roasted."

It almost sounds as if gourmets are willing to talk up *anything*, but that's not so. Roast peacock was the ornate centerpiece of many royal banquets from medieval times through the early eighteenth century. It was expensive and must have looked impressive decorated with its own feathers and breathing flames from a bit of camphor in its gilded beak. No one who tasted it thought it was any good.

A handful of restaurants specialize in the flesh of exotic animals such as hippopotamus and elephant. By all accounts, though, the flesh of animals we don't ordinarily eat tastes not all that different from that of the animals we do eat. More than one jocular memoir of the 1870 siege of Paris describes the flavors of the pets and zoo animals served to the starving population by the city's finest chefs. It's kind of disappointing to learn that hippopotamus tastes like beef; elephant is a little oily; everything on four legs tastes pretty much like pork or chicken or beef. No one thought the flavors were anything exceptional—with the possible exception of cat. César Ritz had kind words for cat meat, and stranded statesman Henry du Pré Labouchère advised, "Don't drown your kittens, eat 'em!"

As it is, eating at a crowded sushi bar entails overhearing at least one graphic description of what happens if you eat raw fish with parasites. Fugu, the most prized delicacy of Japan, is sushi squared. Try this on for size: a toxin 25 times more lethal, weight for weight, than curare with no known antidote. The unbelievably toxic tetrodotoxin resides in the fugu fish's skin, liver, and ovaries. The part of the fish that *won't* kill you is the most prized food of Japan.

Fugu swims in a huge body of tradition and romance only partly comprehensible to those not versed in Japanese culture. Fugu comes from the fish variously known as the puffer, blowfish, or "river pig" in idiomatic Japanese. Found in warm seas the world over, it is the fish that is able to inflate itself when danger threatens, a ruse not entirely successful in preventing it from being made into lamps for Polynesian restaurants. The seventeenth-century poet Basho wrote celebrated haikus about fugu's rare flavor and toxological symptoms. It is also a favored subject of senryu poetry. Japan's emperor is traditionally forbidden to eat fugu.

The perceived danger of eating fugu has contributed to its unparalleled reputation in Japanese gastronomy. What rarity has done for caviar, the toxin has done for fugu. (The fish is not especially rare, though it is becoming overfished in Japan's Inland Sea.) The toxin still claims several lives a year in Japan, mostly from home preparation. Chefs require a special license to prepare fugu in restaurants. Japanese law requires that the viscera be incinerated rather than thrown into the garbage.

The fish's flesh itself is free of toxin. The danger is that the chef's knife may slip during the skinning and gutting and contaminate the flesh. It doesn't take much toxin to kill. Nor can Machiavellian diners play it safe by waiting until everyone else has tried the fugu. A single slice of fugu sashimi may be tainted while the rest is okay; symptoms take hours to show up, anyway. The roster of fugu poisoning symptoms are as nasty as you could ask for, beginning with an anesthetizing tingle about the lips and ending with such complete paralysis as to cause asphyxia while the victim remains fully conscious. In the absence of an antidote, the only treatment is to induce vomiting (in the unlikely event that the bad fugu is recognized immediately) or to rush the victim to a hospital for symptomatic treatment.

Despite the toxicity of the liver, some people have dared to eat it. At a Kyoto restaurant in 1975, popular Kabuki actor Mitsugoro Bando demanded fugu liver for his table. The chef complied, and Bando ate his own portion and those of his four more cautious guests. Bando died that night. The publicity given Bando's death devastated the fugu industry. Prices plummeted to a quarter of their previous levels. The chef was tried for negligence and given an eight-year suspended sentence. The restaurant came to an out-of-court settlement with Bando's heirs for 26 million yen.

In 1980 the U.S. Food and Drug Administration banned the importing of fugu into the United States. A few U.S. restaurants continued to serve fugu during the ban, apparently making do with local puffer fish. In 1989 the FDA lifted the ban.

The most prized type of fugu is that from wild (not artificially cultured) three-year-old tiger puffers. It sells for about $45 a pound at the dock. In Japanese restaurants, a full fugu dinner costs the equivalent of $400. Several ounces of the precious flesh are apportioned into fugu sashimi, fugu stew, miso soup with chunks of fugu, and sake with two grilled fugu fins floating in it.

An early traveler named Dr. Semann wrote: "The pineapple, the mangosteen, and the cherimoya are considered the finest fruits in the world. I have tasted them in those localities in which they are supposed to attain their highest perfection—the pineapple in Guayaquil, the mangosteen in the Indian Archipelago, and the cherimoya on the slopes of the Andes,—and if I were called upon to act the part of a Paris I would without hesitation assign the apple to the cherimoya. Its taste, indeed, surpasses that of every other fruit, and Haenke was quite right when he called it the masterpiece of Nature." The interesting thing is that pineapples caught on, yet most Americans have never seen a mangosteen or a cherimoya.

Semann and Haenke weren't the only ones to speak in favor of cherimoyas. From its representations in their art, the cherimoya seems to have been among the favorite foods of the Incas. Mark Twain tasted a cherimoya and said it was "deliciousness itself." The cherimoya is a melon-sized fruit, rounded or somewhat heart-shaped. The green skin resembles chain-mail armor. The edible flesh is ivory, acquiring a tobacco-stain patina near the skin when ripe. Cherimoya pulp looks like pineapple with large black seeds.

The cherimoya comes from far up in the Andes of Ecuador and Peru and consequently stands cooler temperatures than do other tropical fruits. It is grown on the French Riviera, in southern Spain, Sicily, the Canary and Madeira islands, the West Indies, Mexico, Southern California, and Hawaii. The first cherimoya to fruit in California was planted about 1864 in Santa Barbara. There was once a producing cherimoya grove in Hollywood, California (commemorated with a Cheremoya [sic] Avenue at the base of the Hollywood Hills). Some California growers have planted them recently in reaction to the glutted market for avocados and kiwifruit. In the past decade, the cherimoya has started to show up in American supermarkets and gourmet stores (Balducci's in New York has it seasonally). It costs about $6 a pound.

The other fruit Semann mentioned, the mangosteen, is much harder to come by. The mangosteen is, first of all, not to be confused with the much more common mango. The mango, a green, yellow, or red fruit that is often seen in markets, can be quite good, but it is nothing like the mangosteen (which is unrelated).

Many Americans come across the mangosteen in Japan, where it is perhaps the most popular fruit. "Since the days when early voyagers returned to Europe with more or less fabulous stories of the wonders of the East, the mangosteen has received unstinted praise," reported Wilson Popenoe in 1920, who held the title of Agricultural Explorer for the U.S. Department of Agriculture. "It has been termed the 'Queen of Fruits,' 'the finest fruit in the world,' and Jacobus Bontius, who compared it to nectar and ambrosia, said that it surpassed the golden apples of the Hesperides and was 'of all the fruits of the Indes by far the most delicious.' " It remains little known in the West. The short entry in the *Larousse Gastronomique* describes it only as having "delicious raspberry-flavoured pulp."

The mangosteen is a small fruit tree believed native to the Malay Peninsula and nearby islands. The fruit is about the size of a small tomato, with a dark purple rind. Even botanical descriptions of the mangosteen lapse into thinly veiled eroticism. "The cut surface of the rind is of a moist delicate pink color and is studded with small yellow points formed by the drops of exuding fluid," writes horticulturalist David Fairchild. "As one lifts out of this cup, one by one, the delicate segments, which are the size and shape of those of a mandarin orange, the light pink sides of the cup and the veins of white and yellow embedded in it are visible. The separate segments are between snow white and ivory in color, and are covered with a delicate network of fibers, and the side of each segment where it presses against its neighbor is translucent and slightly tinged with pale green. The texture of the mangosteen pulp much resembles that of a well-ripened plum, only it is so delicate that it melts in the mouth like a bit of ice cream. The flavor is quite indescribably delicious. There is nothing to mar the perfection of this fruit, unless it be that the juice from the rind forms an indelible stain on a white napkin."

Despite the fact that everyone seems to be crazy about it, the mangosteen is nowhere that big a crop and is not exported much beyond the Orient. It was once claimed improbably that the mangosteen tree would grow only within four degrees of the equator. It requires an exacting hot, moist climate and is picky about soil, pruning, and such. Though a favorite with the Japanese, the mangosteen cannot grow in Japan and must be imported from more tropical lands. A few trees have been grown in the West Indies and Hawaii. In 1920 Popenoe stated that the largest mangosteen plantation in the world had no more than 400 trees. That plantation, on the outskirts of Saigon (Ho Chi Minh City), is presumably long gone.

Under refrigeration, mangosteens retain good flavor for as long as a month. When it goes bad, a mangosteen suffers rigor mortis—its rind becomes hard rather than mushy. A mangosteen preserve called halwa manggis is reported to be a poor substitute for the fresh fruit. Canned mangosteens in sugar syrup may be found in New York's Chinatown. Their taste, unfortunately, is little different from that of your basic canned fruit cocktail. We were able to order the whole fruit through an importer in Los Angeles.

What about the plain old pineapple? It's a victim of success. In colonial times, pineapples were rare and expensive, the sort of thing the founding fathers might serve at a state dinner. George Washington is quoted as having judged the Barbados pineapple the finest of tropical fruits. Then pineapple became cheap and contemptibly familiar through Del Monte fruit cocktails and chunks floating in Jell-O. If you have ever had a fresh pineapple in an area where they're grown, or one flown in by jet to market, you know that it is very good indeed. But for most people most of the time, the pineapple is the limp, canned product.

The most controversial of delicacies has to be the durian. It's either the most delicious substance on earth or the worst or both.

"It is of such an excellent taste that it surpasses in flavor all the other fruits of the world, according to those who have tasted it," said the explorer Linschott in 1599. A Dr. Paludanus painted the durian as addictive as lotus fruit: "To those not used to it, it seems at first to smell like rotten onions, but immediately after they have tasted it they prefer it to all other food. The natives give it honorable titles, exalt it, and make verses on it." Durians are the size of honeydew melons, yellowish green, and armed with spines. The spines are so sharp, and the fruit so heavy, that it is difficult to lift a durian if the stalk has broken off. Durian groves are dangerous places. Falling at random moments from high treetops, the massive husk of the durian can kill anyone unlucky enough to be under it. Biologist and explorer Alfred Russel Wallace warns: "When a Durian strikes a man in its fall, it produces a dreadful wound, the strong spines tearing open the flesh, while the blow itself is very heavy; but from this very circumstance death rarely ensues, the copious effusion of blood preventing the inflammation which might otherwise take place."

The woody husk is sometimes difficult to open. Inside are five masses of cream-colored pulp. The pulp is soft and custardy, without juice. It smells just awful. "Because the odor of the durian is repulsive to many, laws, precedents and social customs regulate its movement and storage," say Steven Nagy and Philip E. Shaw in *Tropical and Subtropical Fruits* (1980). Some Asian airlines ban durians on their flights.

Some imply that the bad part is the smell, and if you hold your nose, it's delicious. Novelist Anthony Burgess mentioned "that king of fruits the durian which sheds its delicious fetidity in the season of durians" in *Homage to QWERT YUIOP* (1986). Burgess compared the experience of eating durian to "eating vanilla custard in a latrine." The most famous description of the durian is that of the biologist Wallace in his book *The Malay Archipelago.* "When brought into the house the smell is often so offensive that some persons can never bear to taste it. This was my own case when I first tried it in Malacca, but in Borneo I found a ripe fruit on the ground, and, eating it out of doors, I at once became a confirmed Durian eater . . . its consistence and flavor are indescribable. A rich butter-like custard highly flavored with almonds gives the best general idea of it, but intermingled with it come wafts of flavor that call to mind cream-cheese, onion-sauce, brown sherry, and other incongruities. Then there is a rich glutinous smoothness in the pulp which nothing else possesses, but which adds to its delicacy. It is neither acid, nor sweet, nor juicy, yet one feels the want of none of these qualities, for it is perfect as it is. In fact to eat Durians is a new sensation, worth a voyage to the East to experience. . . . It would not, perhaps, be correct to say that the Durian is the best of all fruits, because it cannot supply the place of the subacid, juicy kinds . . . but as producing a food of the most exquisite flavor it is unsurpassed."

Durians are so popular in Asia that they figure in a wide range of ancillary products. When the pulp is frozen and eaten half thawed, it is said to be something like ice cream. Real ice cream flavored with durian is popular, too. Strict import regulations (durians are a host for medflies), limited demand, and the odor prevent durians from making it to U.S. supermarkets. Fresh durians are seasonally found in some Chinese and Thai markets in the United States.

A modicum of disappointment is built into the idea of a delicacy. Most of the foods that most people like are common. We don't count watermelon and ice cream as delicacies; they're too cheap and available. There is no reason to suppose that the best-tasting foods should also be the rarest and most expensive. Whether animal or vegetable, most foods can be cultivated if only there is a market for them. (The truffle is an unusual exception.)

The confusion of rarest or most expensive with best has occasionally attained the level of self-parody. Herman Melville reported that ordinary salt was the most costly of seasonings in Typee and invested with the snob appeal of a rare Bordeaux. In Brillat-Savarin's time, sugar water, an extravagance then affordable only by Europe's aristocracy, was held in a degree of reverence that is hard to imagine today. Brillat-Savarin recounts: "M. Delacroix . . . complained to me once at Versailles about the price of sugar, which at that time cost more than five francs a pound. 'Ah,' he said in a wistful, tender voice, 'if it can ever again be bought for thirty cents, I'll never more touch water unless it's sweetened!'" Today there are probably people who drink Pepsi with every meal but they're not considered culinary trendsetters for it.

It is easy to be taken in by the presentation or reputation of a food. Anything that is expensive is eaten under different circumstances from other foods. It is more likely to be eaten in a restaurant, on nice plates and linen, and in the company of people who share expectations about it. We wondered if tasters who didn't know what they were tasting would be able to distinguish claimed delicacies from other unfamiliar foods.

The pompous French poet and critic Charles Monselet (1828–88) was the victim of several gastronomical jokes. A prominent restaurateur cajoled Monselet to dinner with promises of rare delicacies. Monselet enjoyed the meal, lecturing on each course. After dessert, his host revealed that the "swallow's nest soup" had been a puree of noodles and kidney beans, the "izard cutlets" were lamb soaked in bitters, and so on. This same Monselet was later invited unknowingly to a gourmet meal in which everything from the "fish" to an omelet was made from the flesh and eggs of a crocodile brought back from Egypt.

For our test, volunteer tasters were blindfolded and asked to sample bite-sized portions of alleged delicacies and more ordinary decoy foods in random order. They did not know, in any particular instance, whether what they were tasting had been touted as the most delicious thing in the world. Most of the time they did not recognize what they were tasting.

The tested foods included a premium beluga malassol caviar, Périgord black truffles, Italian white truffles, cherimoya, mangosteen, and durian. The decoy foods (chosen to be edible but unfamiliar) were Libby's "Potted Meat Food Product," Gerber's "Hawaiian Delight" baby food, kimchee (Korean pickled cabbage), and kiwano (a fruit from New Zealand).

The panelists were asked to rank the nine foods tasted in order of preference. This information was recorded, then the blindfolds were removed. Foods were identified, and the panelists were allowed to try them again and to comment on them. In addition, fugu, grouse, and pheasant were sampled at restaurants. The latter, of course, were not blind comparisons.

The wild card in any sampling of unfamiliar foods is acquired tastes. Everything from caviar to durian is said to taste better with habit. Our test could not allow for that, since most panelists had never tasted any of the object foods before. It is risky to judge a perishable item by a single sample. There's a big difference between the best apple you've ever tasted and one that was mushy and overripe or green and tasteless. We couldn't be absolutely sure that the samples represented the perfection of their kind or whether they were a little off. They all seemed to be fresh or ripe and sound, though.

To rate the foods in the blind tasting, we averaged the numerical rankings (1 is best, 9 is worst) and then ranked by the averages. Practically all the panelists rated nearly all the delicacies better than the decoy foods. The two exceptions were the durian and the cherimoya.

The durian was the *least* preferred of all the foods. Some panelists refused to eat it and could be coaxed only with renewed assurances that the glutinous substance on their spoon was actually edible. Everyone hated it.

The durian is a source of ever-changing odors, most of them unpleasant. The most pervading smell, the one you notice on the other side of the room, is uncannily like the odor the gas company puts in gas so you can detect a leak. The closer you get to durian, the worse it smells. The principal odor close up is like both bubble gum and vomit. Then unexpectedly you get a whiff of hamburger with onions.

Eating durian is one of the oddest of culinary experiences. The first bite was really revolting. The gooey texture, the rubbery skin, and the smell suggest too vividly the sloughing flesh of a decaying animal. Then you hold your breath and take another bite. The durian tastes nothing like a fruit. It is like a very sweet custard or ice cream flavored heavily with green onions, nuts, and meat. Wallace's description is accurate except where he says it isn't sweet. It was extremely sweet.

The best thing about the durian is that, if you can get used to all the weird smells and off flavors, it tastes remarkably like custard. You probably wouldn't think any kind of custard was worth a trip around the world, though. All things considered, you wouldn't like it, much less think it was the best thing you ever tasted.

The panel preferred the cherimoya to all the decoy foods (which were rated, worst to best, as kiwano, kimchee, Hawaiian Delight baby food, and Potted Meat Food Product). No one agreed with Twain that cherimoya was "deliciousness itself." Of the more familiar fruits, the one it most resembles is papaya. It's very sweet, with a perfumey, tutti-frutti, or even "artificial" edge to it. Most found the cherimoya way too sweet. It's not just sugary; it tastes as if there is NutraSweet in there. Aside from that, the flavor was slightly tart, suggesting an interesting mixture of banana, strawberry, pineapple, sour apple, and licorice. There's nothing offensive about the cherimoya; it's just not all that good.

White truffles did much poorer than black with our tasters. They were rated above cherimoya but under caviar. White truffles are really a sandy yellow-brown outside. Inside they are mottled like agate. The texture is smooth. The taste is meatlike with an acrid, garlicky, almost "burnt" flavor. The uniquely white-truffle quality, the flavor that distinguishes it from the black kind, is smoky, earthy, and vaguely reminiscent of paint thinner. They're not as bad as that sounds, but they're a little strong for eating alone, as in our test. White truffles might go further than black ones as a pricey imposition in pâtés or pasta.

Caviar, too, is normally a quasi garnish. The panelists tried it with no accompaniments, which may not be the best indication of how it would taste with blinis and sour cream or with chopped egg and lemon. Further, this was the one food that most of the panelists said they recognized in the blind tasting. The tasters felt that the vaunted fresh golden caviar was not a completely different animal from the more familiar kind. It looked good. It was composed of perfect buckshot-size roe of a greenish-sepia color. The flavor was still distinctly salty (if less so than the pasteurized kind). It was still fishy. The difference was that it also had more of the flavor of unspoiled fish. If you like preserved caviar, you'll like this. You may not feel the difference is like day and night. If you think the cheap stuff is fishy and salty and awful, you'll think this is, too. Many of our tasters like the bargain-brand caviars, so this got a good rating overall. Many felt, however, that it was no better than a good deli salmon or lox.

Black truffles are delicious. They were much preferred to white truffles and to caviar. The flavor is less astringent than that of white truffles. It's not much like anything else. You could say it's something like steak and coconut, with overtones of soup and tar, but that doesn't begin to describe it. The texture is pleasantly gritty, like a pear's.

The most preferred food was the mangosteen. Nearly everyone rated it in the top three. The white segments have a watermelonlike texture. The taste is pleasantly complex. Like most fruits, the mangosteen's taste is a mixture of sweet and sour. It has a distinctive character that some described as "green"—a slight bittersweet aftertaste that is very refreshing. It is different from anything you've ever tasted, and it is very good indeed.

Grouse and pheasant, sampled at restaurants, provided no surprises. They were good, not radically different from duck. Fugu sashimi was the most profoundly disappointing food tasted. There was nothing wrong with it; it was just a mouthful of *nothing*.

The thin slices of translucent white fugu were presented

nicely, with garnishes that looked more interesting than the fugu did. It was almost tasteless. It was a little sweet, and a little fishy—that's about it. The rubbery, almost gristlelike texture was more notable than the flavor. It was like what people who won't eat sashimi think sashimi is like. All told, fugu was not nearly as tasty as garden-variety sashimi made from tuna, yellowtail, or eel.

None of the foods tested was overwhelmingly the best thing that anyone had ever tasted. Everyone could name something (like chocolate truffle or lobster) that they liked as much as the best thing in the tasting. But in case you're curious from years of hearing about this stuff, here's an idea of what to expect:

You'd gag on durian. You would have no trouble downing fugu if you like sashimi, but wouldn't find it anything special. You wouldn't like cherimoya much.

You might or might not like golden caviar or white truffles. Grouse and pheasant taste just about like what you'd imagine.

You'd love black truffles and mangosteens.

# THE BEST
# TYPE OF
# AUDIO
# RECORDING

# CD, LP, OR TAPE?

No matter which you listen to, some people think you're pathetically misguided. Not everyone hails the digital age. Even as chain stores drop LPs altogether, even as record companies release albums in CD and cassette formats solely, debate rages over the merits of compact discs, the digital wonders that everyone told us to buy. A vocal and influential backlash of audiophiles bemoans the (take your pick) harsh, sterile, grainy, empty, two-dimensional, dry, and generally *je ne sais quoi*–deficient digital sound. They hold that LPs are still the only choice for the true music lover.

Lacking a claque are tapes, still the most convenient medium of all. It is widely asserted that all commercial cassette releases are lousy; that you should dub your own from CD or LP. Dubbed tapes presumably acquire the defects, real or imagined, of their source.

Much of the contention revolves around the distinction between digital and analog recordings. In 1986 Harry Pearson, editor of *Absolute Sound,* a pro-analog newsletter, informed *Time* magazine that digital sound is "metallic, gritty, grainy and unnatural." Pearson said, "The woodwinds all sound alike. You can't tell the difference between one string and another, and you can't tell if what you're hearing is a horn or a trumpet. Digital audio is like McDonald's hamburgers. It's all alike."

"What is appalling about digital sound is the lack of musicality," explained CD trasher Michael Tapes of Sound Workshop Professional Audio Products in *Stereo Review* (1984). "It subtracts the essence of music. If you listen to an analog recording and a digital one, the brain responds positively to the analog and negatively to the digital. Music is an emotional medium, and it's the emotion that digital takes out."

*Stereo Review* columnist Ralph Hodges quoted an unnamed enthusiast in 1985: "The digital process is antiseptic, and it kills the microbes of the sound that are a part of all organic life . . . It's dead."

All this runs counter to the familiar line that the CD is, well, "the greatest advance in home sound reproduction since the switch from the acoustic to the electrically amplified phonograph." Julian Hirsch of Hirsch-Houck Labs put it that way in a 1984 issue of *Stereo Review. Consumer Reports* (1985) told its value-conscious readers, "In theory a CD system is inherently capable of delivering high-quality sound reproduction. But we were simply not prepared for the uniformly excellent performance of these players. By every criterion we used, the players were far superior to any sound-reproduction device we have ever tested."

There is a whiff of elitism in the CD vs. LP argument. The

analog guys are mostly those who can afford to spend a lot of money on the best equipment. More than that, they're mostly people who have already shelled out a lot of money for the best analog equipment. The argument goes: Sure a CD is a good buy if all you've got is a few hundred dollars to spend. But you should hear a record on a $1,000 cartridge connected to a $10,000 turntable system. The digital faction grumbles that it can't hear any difference, that it's a case of the emperor's new clothes, and anyway, digital sound is perfect, period. Depending on your sympathies, the analog people are trying to justify all the money they spent, or the CD people are crying sour grapes. As in the movie colorization debate, a passionate elite looks down at the masses who embrace the latest techno-vulgarity. The difference is that everyone agrees a colorized movie is *different* from a black-and-white one. Not everyone is sure there's an audible difference between digital and analog sound.

The digital dispute is the most frequently voiced example of an audiophile fetish, the technological superstitions of stereo nuts. There used to be arguments over sapphire vs. diamond needles and over integrated circuits vs. good old-fashioned transistors. The diamond needles and the discrete transistors were supposed to produce better sound—no one was quite sure how or why. The integrated-circuit issue fell by the wayside as everyone adopted integrated circuits. It has been replaced by other points of contention equally arcane. Some listeners think that having a digital watch in the room with a stereo wrecks the sound, somehow. Some say a telephone has the same effect.

A lot of these fetishes have more to do with the psychology of audiophiles than with either music or electronics. That does not mean that the analog purists are wrong. From a technical standpoint, the analog fetish is among the more respectable. Digital recording is relatively new at the consumer level, and it is fundamentally different from analog recording. There is reasonable concern about whether, and to what extent, the differences are audible and capable of impairing the listening experience.

Understand what we're talking about. No one disputes that a CD or digital audio tape (DAT) has far less noise than a phonograph record or regular tape. The surface noise, the turntable rumble, and slight pitch fluctuations are absent. That permits a higher dynamic range. You can hear the long, slow fade-out of a cymbal crash. No one disputes that the cleaner sound is all for the good.

The argument concerns the quality of the music itself. Purists say that the analog recordings are in some respect richer or more faithful to the original music than digital recordings are. Three common explanations for the alleged inferiority of digital sound are worth mentioning. One is error correction. An analog recording has a direct impression of the original music. A CD player is a kind of computer that reads a lot of 1s and 0s from the disc and reconstitutes them into the music. Sometimes the player reads the encoded data incorrectly. This is most common with a poorly manufactured CD or one with scratches, fingerprints, or warps. When that happens, the player tries to correct for the error. If just a single bit here and there is misread, the player can correct for it perfectly through clever design. This, all sound engineers insist, shouldn't make any difference whatsoever in sound quality.

When too many nearby bits are unreadable, the player *interpolates:* It makes a "guess" about the missing data. The guess is rarely right on the mark. Repeated interpolations, as from a badly damaged disc, are audible as a clicking sound. Some analog partisans charge that even the occasional interpolation that might occur in a good CD has a deleterious effect on the music.

Philips and Sony, the licensers of the CD technology, monitor the number of errors in pressings. It is required that a new disc have no more than 220 errors per second. That sounds enormously high, but normally all of these would be error-corrected. Most discs considerably better this standard. According to a test by David Ranada reported in *High Fidelity,* "Nowadays, you will have to play at least 20 new CDs to find even one interpolated data block . . . [Interpolation] is rare even with fingerprinted and scratched discs: If they play at all, then they are being fully and exactly error-corrected."

CDs cannot reproduce some very high notes. The limit for CDs is about 20,000 Hz. Phonographs can reproduce notes several times higher. However, the CD limit is not necessarily a problem, because the limit of the average person's hearing is about 20,000 Hz also. As people age, the upper-frequency limit of hearing decreases. Old people can't hear high notes they could when they were younger. Conceivably, older listeners might find a CD fine while younger ones would find something missing. (In reality, it's not the kids who demand analog and the old folks who are happy with digital—it's usually the other way around.) The strongest practical argument for the CD's acceptability is FM radio. The frequency limit of the FM process is about 15,000 Hz, well under the CD ceiling. No one seems to complain much about that cutoff. Still, it is difficult to be sure that "inaudible" notes and overtones make no contribution to the listening experience.

The third point is least controversial. Early CD releases had undeniable defects. Recording is a complicated business, and CDs demand different recording techniques from LPs. "Preemphasis" of high notes is necessary lest faint high tones be lost. It took some time for engineers to get the hang of the new medium. The exaggerated "brilliance" of the early CDs has been reduced, perhaps eliminated, with new microphone placements. A popular argument with more sophisticated CD apologists is that any defects of the CD are due to bad microphone placements and other misjudgments on the part of sound engineers. The CD is so good at reproducing sound, these people say, that these human errors are duly reproduced. The other side charges that "bad miking" is just a handy excuse for the medium's failings.

Some CDs, especially of vintage classical performances, were created from the old analog tapes. Thus you get a digital reproduction of the analog recording, complete with hiss. Essentially all new releases are digitally recorded and mastered (and so identified by the "DDD" on the label).

Direct listening comparisons between analog and digital recordings are dubious. It wouldn't do simply to put an audio system behind a curtain and switch the speakers between a CD player, a tape deck, and a turntable. The crackle would betray the turntable; listeners might vote their prejudices. Even with the most costly analog equipment, which comes close to CD players in noise level, there is usually a telltale click or two at the beginning of the record.

We conducted the following double-blind test. A panel of listeners were assembled to audition selections of music and compare the quality of reproduction. The sound system was out of sight behind a partition. We used the commercial analog and digital releases of Glenn Gould's recording of Bach's *Goldberg Variations* (CBS, 1956 & 1983). The CD is not a fully digital product (DDD). It is "ADD": Gould's session performance was recorded on *analog* tape back in 1955, it was remastered for the CD on a *digital* tape recorder, and of course the final product, the CD itself, is *digital.* Thus the CD reproduces the very same recording as the LP and the tape do. Even the CD retains the noise and other earmarks of the original analog tape.

An ADD recording is hardly the best representative of the digital medium's virtues. It should have all the medium's vices. If something bad happens to music in sampling it at 44,100 times a second, breaking it down into bits, and encoding it as pits in an aluminum and plastic disc, then an ADD recording should be as much heir to these evils as a DDD recording.

As played, the CD still comes out cleaner-sounding than the analog recordings. That's because phonographs and tape decks generate their own noise in addition to that inherent in the recording. To even things out, we created a noise tape by recording the telltale initial crackle from a phonograph on regular, analog tape. The rest of the tape was blank. Playing the blank part of the noise tape produced a small amount of background hiss as well as the sound of the tape drive itself. Part of the time, this noise tape was cued and played simultaneously on a separate tape deck and speakers with music from a CD player. Both systems were behind a partition, out of sight of the listeners. Thus, part of the time the listeners heard CD digital music *with phonograph and tape noise.*

The listeners heard seven types of sources played at identical volume. They included four varieties of recorded music you're likely to find in your home or car: phonograph recordings, commercial tape recordings, tapes made from a CD, and CDs. Of these, the CD is digital, and the tape made from the CD is an analog recording from a digital source. The other sources were analog. (DATs were not tested. In theory, they should produce the same results as CDs.)

The panel also heard the CD masked with the noise tape. The CD signal (which has relatively modest dynamic range in the Gould recording) was played simultaneously with the noise tape. This should be a stringent test of listeners' ability to discriminate between digital and analog sound. The listeners were aware that some sources would be disguised in various ways but did not, of course, know which selection came from which player.

Setting up selections required punching some noisy buttons on the tape deck. To minimize the chance of listeners unconsciously surmising sources from the sounds of setup, we made sure to punch some button, even if not necessary, before each selection. Radio music was played between selections to mask setup sounds further.

A trial run showed that some of the sources were difficult to distinguish. There is no point in asking listeners which source they prefer if they cannot even tell which is which. We therefore used a so-called ABX comparison. For each trial, three short passages of music were played. The first passage (say from a CD player masked with noise) would be called source A; the second would be source B (which might be a phonograph record); the third would be from mystery source X—either the same as A or the same as B. The listeners were asked to identify which of the first two sources was identical to the last. They were also asked which source (A or B) they preferred. For uniformity, they were required to state a preference even if it was slight or even if they really had no preference. Each trio of sources was played twice to help listeners make up their minds.

Listeners recorded their guess about source X and their preference on a tally sheet. "AB" would mean that the third source sounded like the first (A) and that the listener preferred the second (B) to the first. Sources A and B varied from trial to trial, as did the identity of source X. The order of the passages and so forth was preselected randomly. However, sources A and B were always different, and X was always the same as one of them. Ten sets of three passages were auditioned. This allowed each of the five sources to be compared with every other source.

It stands to reason that if listeners could not even *distinguish* one source from another, they could hardly have a genuine preference. By pure chance, you would expect half the panelists to correctly identify source X. So when the identification rate is about 50 percent, the preferences must be judged doubtful. A meaningful result would be for most of the listeners to identify source X correctly *and* for them to prefer one of the two sources. The results were as follows:

*LP vs. commercial tape.* Seven of ten panelists correctly identified the third source. Remember, you would expect five to make the identification by pure luck, so this is a moderate degree of discrimination. Six of the ten preferred the LP. That's an insubstantial victory for the LP over the tape.

*LP vs. tape made from CD.* Seven out of ten identified source X, and five preferred the LP. There was no net preference.

*Tape vs. tape made from CD.* Only four panelists identified source X, less than you'd expect from random guessing. That invalidates the preferences, which were close anyway (six favored the commercial tape). If this test is any indication, CD-dubbed tapes are just as good (or as bad) as commercial tapes. (The test used a single cassette and was not designed to indicate a quality-control problem that might result in some good tapes and some defective ones.)

*LP vs. CD.* No surprise here—eight out of ten identified source X, and nine preferred the CD. We did not seek to recruit digital partisans for the panel, and it is unlikely that this is atypical of the listening public.

*Tape vs. CD.* Seven distinguished the sources, and seven preferred the CD.

*Tape made from CD vs. CD.* Eight out of ten distinguished the sources, and seven preferred the CD.

*CD vs. masked CD.* Only one listener failed to distinguish the CD from the CD with the noise, and everyone preferred the CD.

Now for the crux of the comparison:

*LP vs. masked CD.* Six correctly distinguished the sources. That's well within the range of chance. The preferences were split exactly evenly.

*Tape vs. masked CD.* Five distinguished the sources, just what you'd expect if people were guessing blindly. Five said they preferred the tape.

*Tape made from CD vs. masked CD.* Seven distinguished the sources, and six preferred the CD.

The big surprise was how similar the CD, tape, and LP

sounded, at least in this special case of a CD made from an analog recording. Our listeners did not find grittiness, graininess, or absence of "microbes of the sound" in the CD's music. There is little if any indication that they could distinguish analog music from digital at all, except by the analog source's admitted failings. When these failings were simulated, the digital source sounded the same. We found no reason to avoid CDs and their undisputed advantages.

# THE MOST PROFITABLE INVESTMENT

# IN 1985

*Money* magazine reported that the original Barbie doll, released in 1959, was selling for about $500 each. And don't even think about shampooing the dog with that old bottle of Ringo Starr bubble bath—it was worth about $85. It's easy to laugh this off until you do a little math and realize that the price appreciation for Barbie dolls and Ringo shampoos has exceeded 20 percent per year. Chances are, your pension fund didn't do nearly that well.

It's claims like this that turn traditional investment advice on its head. A 1989 ad touting American Eagle gold coins in *The Wall Street Journal* states, "Throughout civilized history, gold has been one of the most precious investments individuals and governments can make. . . . In fact, gold's performance over time has been competitive with stocks, bonds and real estate." *Money* magazine noted that Australia's Gold Nugget coins jumped from $1,435 to $2,100 (a 46 percent gain) in a single year's time (late 1986 to 1987).

From 1974 to 1980, the average price of a one-carat D-flawless diamond zoomed from $4,300 to $62,000, said *U.S. News & World Report* (1984). That's a 14-fold increase and a 56 percent annual return.

The value of a set of Graf Zeppelin stamps shot from $1,700 to "between $2,500 and $3,000" in 1987 *(U.S. News & World Report,* 1987). This is about a 60 percent gain in a single year.

According to *Connoisseur* magazine (1988), the average auction prices of paintings by Renoir went up 490 percent in the period 1975 to 1987. Monet's prices went up 440 percent in the same period, and Degas's, 350 percent.

The *Guinness Book of World Records* credits Pennzoil with the largest single-day increase of an actively traded stock. On December 10, 1985, Pennzoil stock rose from 19 3/4 to 83. Pennzoil options (contracts to buy the stock at a fixed price) fared better yet. They shot from $375 to $10,250 that same day, a 27-fold increase and "the fastest gain in history" according to the Guinness book.

Well, you get the idea. People go on and on, and *it doesn't prove anything.* Sure, if you had known to buy Pennzoil options on that particular day, you could have made a killing. Had you known to pick a certain lottery number, you could have won. The question is whether you could have reasonably selected the investment based on information available at the time and staked your life savings on it. If not, the performance is irrelevant.

It is easy to be cynical about the whole business, but some

investments *are* better than others. Two ground rules help make sense of the welter of claims littering cocktail parties and investment pitches. The first rule is to beware of hindsight. Ignore claims of how much money you could have made by knowing which *specific* investment vehicles to buy. You can't expect to pick the next Xerox, except as part of a portfolio of growth stocks that will inevitably include losers and winners. We will consider general classes of investments only.

The second rule is to keep things simple. It is hard to keep track of all the numbers cited in proof of an investment's performance. Is a bottle of Beatles bubble bath that appreciated from $1 in 1965 to $85 in 1985 better or worse than something that doubles your money in five years? We need a single number telling how good an investment is. Of course, the number has to permit direct comparisons of one investment with another.

The most widely used number is the annual return. You punch a few figures into a financial calculator and out pops a percentage telling how much the investment increased each year. Saying that something has an annual return of 7 percent means that every dollar invested increased at the same rate as if it were in a savings account that paid 7 percent compound interest. Keeping money as cash provides a return of zero, and bank savings accounts pay about 5 percent. A real investment has to do better than that, or it's not worth the risk.

You can't compare any annual return with any other, though. A return of 10 percent in a bull market is not the same as a 10 percent return during a depression. Besides, any investment does well some of the time. It is easy to select a few good years and compute an annual return worthy of boiler-room telemarketing. Stories of killings get repeated long after prices have dropped precipitously.

To compare widely different investments, annual returns should be computed from the same time period. Better yet, it should be the same *long* period, spanning several business cycles.

Roger G. Ibbotson's *Stocks, Bonds, Bills, and Inflation: Historical Returns (1926–1987)*, published by Dow Jones–Irwin, records stock and bond performance. Since its tabulation predates the Great Depression, it is a decent indication of the historic record. Let's use the six-decade period of the Ibbotson accounting as the basis for comparison. For each investment, we will start with the value in 1926 (or as close to that year as possible) and compare it with the value in or about 1987. The appreciation will be translated into an annual rate of return. Then there will be no question about whether returns reflect performance under different economic conditions.

According to *Stocks, Bonds, Bills, and Inflation,* every dollar invested in 1926 (and reinvested as necessary) in a hypothetical portfolio of 20-year treasury bonds would have grown to $13.35 by the end of 1987. A 13.35-fold increase in 61 years is equivalent to a 4.27 percent annual return, not adjusted for inflation.

Stocks have done a lot better. A dollar invested in the stocks of the Standard & Poor 500 Index in 1926 would have grown to $347.96 in 1987. That's a 9.90 percent annual return.

Many particular stocks did much better in the period since 1926. Again, that is beside the point. The 9.90 percent return applies to a portfolio of well-known companies in the S&P Index. It would have taken no particular cleverness or foresight to invest in them.

You can do better with stocks, even lacking ESP or insider information. While broader than the Dow-Jones Index, the S&P 500 is composed of the largest, most widely traded companies in the country. Most of these companies have passed the meteoric phase of their growth. According to *Stocks, Bonds, Bills, and Inflation,* a dollar invested in 1926 in the smaller companies of the New York and American exchanges and the over-the-counter market would have grown to $1,202.97 by 1987.

Buying "small stocks" is still fair investment advice. You don't have to know *which* small companies to buy. Just buy a representative selection, as some mutual funds do. It will include "right" ones and "wrong" ones. Averaged out, the return is likely to be better than that of big-company stocks. The 1,203-fold increase in 62 years amounts to an annual return of 12.12 percent.

The experts who manage mutual funds, pension funds, or insurance company investments try to top this. Many do better than the averages over periods of a few years. There is scant evidence, however, that any investment philosophy beats the average for small stocks in the long run. The market system works against exceptional returns. Companies with better-than-average promise command higher prices for their stock, bringing their expected return into line with the rest of the market. Better returns are pure luck.

So the question is: Can anything top the long-term 12 percent return of small-company stocks?

Let's start with the most popular investment, real estate. Brokers like to repeat such chestnuts as that of Morton F. Plant, the New York millionaire who traded his Fifth Avenue mansion to Cartier's for a pearl necklace in 1917. The necklace was valued at $1.2 million back then. According to a 1989 article in the *Houston Post,* the necklace is worth only about $200,000 today while the mansion is worth about $20 million. However clear the moral, it doesn't say all that much for real estate as an investment. Assuming Plant made a fair trade, his mansion has appreciated only 17-fold in 72 years, and that is not quite a 4 percent return. That's less than the interest rate on a renter's cleaning deposit these days.

Fifth Avenue was as exclusive an address back then as it is now. You could have done better investing in an area before it became expensive. When Beverly Hills was subdivided in 1906, lots in the 500 blocks just north of Santa Monica Boulevard sold for $900 each. There are no unimproved lots there now, but the real estate is so expensive that the value of smaller houses rests mostly in the land. Buyers often purchase a house just to tear it down and build anew. According to a survey of real estate agents, the current minimum price for a house in the 500 blocks, even for a tear-down, is about $1.7 million. That is an increase of 1,889 times over a period of 83 years. Impressive as this sounds, it works out to only a respectable 9.51 percent annual rate of return. And you would have to knock off a variable amount (probably a few percent) to cover real estate taxes and brokerage fees.

It is questionable if this is a fair example. Beverly Hills was a gamble back then. No matter—even giving it the benefit of the doubt, real estate has not done as well as stocks.

This is not the whole story on real estate. There is little argument that home ownership can be a good investment. It can be much more profitable than other real estate investments because of the leverage and favored tax treatment available to those taking out a mortgage. Is it better than the stock market?

A home is usually purchased with a small down payment and a large loan. This entitles the buyer to the full amount of any appreciation in the property's worth. Such leverage increases the effective return, and may pay off spectacularly in good years in "hot" markets. The flip side of this advantage is the possibility of losing more than your down payment should real estate prices go down. Mortgage interest is also tax-deductible, and this increases the effective return as well.

Neither leverage nor tax benefits are unique to real estate. Investors who buy stock on margin get leverage; investors in some mutual bonds and retirement plans get tax benefits. But it would be wrong to assume that things even out. While you can buy stocks or almost any other investment on credit, it is much easier to buy real estate with a small down payment because of lenders' belief that land rarely decreases in value. There are strict limits on margin purchases of stock; on the other hand, houses are typically purchased with a 20 percent down payment or less.

Let's start with the case of a cash purchase. If you buy a house with cash, there is no leverage and no mortgage tax deduction. Nor are there mortgage payments. You do owe brokerage fees, property taxes, insurance, and upkeep costs. In return you get to live in the house and save on rent.

A 6 percent brokerage fee is standard in most places. Although this is a one-time cost, the average homeowner moves every seven years or so, so it can amount to about 1 percent of the property's value per year. Paying 2 percent of a property's value in taxes and insurance each year is typical. Upkeep and depreciation are partly hidden costs since most homeowners do some of their own repairs. The Internal Revenue Service allows a class life of 27.5 years for computing depreciation on some real property. Assume that everything in the house has to be replaced every 27.5 years, and that half the property's value is in land (which doesn't depreciate). Then the cost of upkeep might be pegged at 1.8 percent of the property's value per year. The total cost of broker fees, taxes, insurance, and upkeep would be 4.8 percent of the property's value—4.8 percent *each year*.

On the plus side is the rental value of the property, or the amount you would have paid on rent for similar accommodations. A real estate rule of thumb is that 1 percent of a property's value is a reasonable monthly rent. Annual rental would be 12 percent of the property's value, but a couple of percentage points are usually deducted to allow for vacancies and the work of renting it out. That leaves 10 percent as the effective rental value.

A house that generates 10 percent of its value in saved rent, less 4.8 percent in expenses, has a net return of 5.2 percent. This is on top of any increase in value. The increase is likely to be around 4 percent in a stable neighborhood. It could be as much as 9.5 percent in special cases (Beverly Hills from subdivision to present). The total return is probably around 9.2 percent, though it could be as high as 14.7 percent.

This return is nothing special, particularly if you discount the Beverly Hills figure as a case of hindsight. It is leverage and tax deductions that make home ownership attractive. To pull some representative figures out of the air, suppose you take out an 80 percent mortgage at 10 percent interest and are in the 28 percent tax bracket. Then you initially pay 8 percent of the property's value in interest each year, and this saves you 2.24 percent of the property's value in taxes. That boosts the effective return to the range 11.4 to about 16.9 percent.

The biggest advantage comes from leverage. An 80 percent mortgage magnifies a property's price appreciation, relative to the 20 percent down payment, by a factor of five. Taking a conservative appreciation rate of 4 percent, leverage raises the appreciation to about 20 percent (16 extra points). That makes the effective return at least 27 percent in the early years of the loan (as much as 55 percent based on the long-term Beverly Hills appreciation rate of 9.5 percent).

There is no denying that tax laws and the banking system stack the deck in favor of *heavily mortgaged* home ownership. When these factors are considered, it is almost impossible to beat the return on owning a home—during the early years of a mortgage, anyway. However, both the mortgage deductions and the leverage diminish as the loan is paid off and the homeowner's equity increases. In the last years of a mortgage, the true return on equity is likely to dip below that of small stocks.

Other investment vehicles promise even higher returns. Try gold. In 1926 an ounce of gold went for about $20.50. By 1980 an ounce went for a record $850. Then its value fell, and in 1989 gold was worth about $384 an ounce. That means the value of gold has increased 19-fold in the same period that the S&P 500 stocks have increased 348-fold. The average annual return of gold bullion has been just 4.76 percent.

Gold coins not only increase in value with the price of gold but also have numismatic value. In the 1920s, you could get an American double eagle gold coin for its face value of $20. Today these widely touted investment coins can sell for as much as $120,000—for a specific rare issue in uncirculated condition. Also, that's what you'd pay to buy it from a dealer, not what a dealer would pay you for it. For a typical coin from the mid-1920s, a dealer would pay about $450. That's only marginally more than the bullion value of the gold. The long-term return has been just over 5 percent.

Silver has not done as well as gold. Its appreciation has averaged under 4 percent over the past 60 years.

In the mid-1920s, a flawless white one-carat diamond was worth about $157. After peaking in 1980, diamond prices dropped like a rock. Recently, one-carat diamonds have been selling for about $15,000. That works out to a historic appreciation of about 8.17 percent.

Though volatile, some rare stamps have appreciated strongly over several business cycles. Only a single sheet of the famous "upside-down airplane" stamps (1918 airmail series, 24 cents) was released. Collector William T. Robey bought the sheet of 100 stamps at the face value of $24 at a Washington post office. When he discovered the error, the post office tried to buy the sheet back. Robey refused. The post office quickly notified other branches to look out for the error, but none were found. Robey realized that he was the owner of a very valuable sheet.

It was a stroke of luck that Robey was in the right post office at the right time to buy the stamps at face value. But consider the appreciation *after* the stamps' rarity was fully realized. Robey was flooded with offers for his sheet and sold it to Philadelphia dealer Eugene Klein for $15,000 ($150 per stamp). The sheet was then broken up and sold. In 1989 a block of four of the stamps went on the auction block in New York and fetched a record $1.1 million. That works out to $275,000 per stamp, an 1,833-fold increase over the price Klein paid. The annual return has been a 11.16 percent. That's better than the S&P 500, but still not as good as the return of small stocks in the same period.

Skyrocketing prices paid for art in recent years have drawn professional money managers into the market. In 1989 New York philanthropist Chauncey D. Stillman sold Pontormo's *Portrait of Cosimo I de' Medici* to the J. Paul Getty Museum for $35.2 million. That was the most ever paid for any old master painting, and it seemed to epitomize the tulipmania-like insanity of the art market. Stillman had purchased the painting for a mere $37,000 in 1927. A little math shows that the annual appreciation was an impressive 11.7 percent. Again, that's better than S&P stocks, though not so good as small stocks.

It is difficult to rate the investment value of collectible kitsch.

Barbie dolls and Beatles memorabilia do not have a long enough track record to be compared with other investments. No one expects Beatles memorabilia to increase geometrically in value for ever and ever. Eventually everyone who has fond memories of the Beatles will be dead and the stuff may be worthless. Not that that would be a problem *if* you could sell it at the peak (just about now?) and reinvest the money in something else. A 20 percent return over two decades (which is presently typical) isn't bad.

It is unclear how much of this return is due to luck. In hindsight, you can fantasize about having bought a warehouseful of Beatles memorabilia. Had you actually tried something like that, you might have stocked up on Chad and Jeremy junk instead. In any case, this does not meet our standards for long-term appreciation. Beatles memorabilia has done well because the 1960s generation has grown both nostalgic and affluent. It does not follow that every generation will be able or willing to pay so much for its memories.

Mickey Mouse toys have a longer record of appreciation. The earliest dolls and watches were produced in the 1930s and sold for around a dollar. Their values now depend on condition and rarity. A typical example is the Fun-E-Flex dolls of Mickey, Minnie, and Pluto distributed by George Borgfeldt beginning in 1931. The *Official Price Guide to Toys* (1988) lists their worth as $100 to $125. That translates into an annual return of less than 9 percent. That's not so remarkable, and it overstates the case. The prices in the *Official Price Guide* are theoretical sale prices to a willing buyer. People willing to pay largish sums of money for old toys are not so easy to find. Dealers and auction houses are likely to pay a seller only half to two-thirds of the listed price, and that for a flawless specimen. Wear and defects lower the price further. All this could reduce the real return to around 7 percent.

One type of collectible has appreciated staggeringly well over a long period: rare comic books. According to the *Official Overstreet Comic Book Price Guide, Detective 27,* published in 1939, is now worth about $35,000. *Marvel Comics No. 1,* also of 1939 vintage, sells for similar amounts. These increases work out to roughly a 30 percent annual return over a 50-year period. *Marvel Comics No. 1* has done much, much better than the stock market over the past half century.

The catch is: These particular issues are valuable because they introduced Batman and Superman. Other comic books from the period have no great value. Anyone who had the clairvoyance to recognize the long-term appeal of Batman or Superman could just as well have known to buy Xerox.

The annual returns look like this:

| | Period | Bought for | Sold for | Return |
|---|---|---|---|---|
| Stocks (small capitalization) | 1926–88 | | | 12.12% |
| Art (Pontormo's *Portrait of Cosimo I de' Medici*) | 1927–89 | $37,000 | $35,200,000 | 11.70% |
| Rare stamps (1918 "upside-down airplane") | 1918–89 | $150 | $275,000 | 11.16% |
| Stocks (S&P 500) | 1926–88 | | | 9.90% |
| Real estate (Beverly Hills, 500 block north of Santa Monica Blvd.) | 1906–89 | $900 | $1,700,000 | 9.51% |
| Mickey Mouse toys (Fun-E-Flex) | 1931–88 | $1.00 | $125 | 8.84% |
| Diamonds (one-carat white flawless) | 1926–84 | $157 | $15,000 | 8.17% |
| Gold coins (U.S. eagles, fine) | 1926–88 | $20 | $450 | 5.15% |
| Gold (ounce) | 1926–89 | $21 | $384 | 4.76% |
| Bonds (20-year U.S. Treasury) | 1926–88 | | | 4.27% |
| Silver (ounce) | 1928–89 | $0.50 | $5.23 | 3.92% |
| Cash | | | | 0.00% |

The verdict: Once you factor out luck, it is doubtful that *any* investment outperforms small stocks over the long term. There is a logic to that. If land or stamps or pop star memorabilia or anything else could be expected, before the fact, to yield a better return than stocks, then people would start issuing stock in syndicates investing in these collectibles.

# THE
# TALLEST
# BUILDING

# YOU'D THINK THAT

the world's tallest building would be beyond dispute. It's the Sears Tower, right? Wrong—*it's a building you've never heard of.* But such is the never-say-die world of tourism that not only the Sears Tower but several shorter buildings rake in visitor dollars on the strength of claims of being the biggest building in the world depending on how you measure it. Even the Empire State Building isn't out of the running. Its management claims that a trip to its glass-enclosed observatory is "an experience which has no parallel anywhere." Perhaps not, but people on the World Trade Center's observation deck are also on top of a tall building in New York, only 112 feet higher.

Height is not the only measurement of how "big" a building is. The tallest building need not necessarily have the greatest area, the greatest volume, or the greatest number of people working or living in it. In fact, four different buildings are number one in height, area, volume, and population, and promoters of at least two claim that makes theirs the biggest building in the world.

The building with the greatest area is believed to be a tank factory in the Soviet Union, the Nizhni Tagil Railroad Car and Tank Plant. It has over 204 acres of floor space, nearly one-quarter the area of Central Park.

The building with the biggest volume is Boeing's main assembly plant in Everett, Washington, the place where 747s come from. The Boeing plant has a volume of roughly 200 million cubic feet, which is nearly three times that of the Pentagon (77 million cubic feet).

The Pentagon is first in population. About 23,000 people work there during the peak daytime hours, roughly the population of Laramie, Wyoming. The Sears Tower houses only about 13,000 workers, half of them working for Sears.

Okay. For most people, height is the only thing that counts. There are more pretenders to the title of world's tallest building than to most voluminous or most populous, and some of the claimants have no merit whatsoever.

A case in point is the Tokyo Tower, the purest, most mercenary of tall buildings. Places like the Sears Tower and the World Trade Center are regular office buildings that happen to be tall. The Tokyo Tower was built just to be tall and attract tourists. That's its only purpose, aside from being a broadcast antenna. It's also a guileless rip-off of the Eiffel Tower—only bigger! "The distance of the tower to the observation deck alone makes it the highest in the world," is a typical claim from the Japan Travel Bureau's English-language guidebook, *A Look into Tokyo* (1987). That's *completely wrong*. Measured from the small building at the base (containing a wax museum with effigies of Japanese stars) to its top, the Tokyo Tower is just 1,093 feet tall. That's not extraordinary, nor is the height of the higher of two observation decks (820 feet). It's the tallest building in Tokyo, that's all.

The Empire State Building *should* be the tallest building in the world. It is the most architecturally distinguished of the biggies, and it gets in the most movies. When it was built, the Empire State Building was touted as one of the wonders of the world—a safe claim to make in the absence of an official world wonders nominating board. The American Society of Civil Engineers hedged their bets somewhat by voting the Empire State Building one of the "Seven Modern Wonders of the Western Hemisphere." An exhibit still in the lobby illustrates the seven wonders of the ancient world—the Colossus of Rhodes, the Hanging Gardens of Babylon, and so on—plus the "Eighth Wonder of the Modern World," the Empire State Building. The building's brochure would have you believe that the Empire State Building is tops in weird phenomena, too: "Snow & rain can be seen falling up! Rain is sometimes red!" Don't count on seeing that, or the promised "Shocking kisses (due to atmospheric conditions)." The building is also the subject of endless silly bets about how much it sways (about an inch even in hurricane-force winds; the building's management is regularly asked to decide wagers claiming as much as 20 feet) or how often it is struck by lightning (a lot).

The trouble is, the World Trade Center is a good 100 feet and eight stories higher than the Empire State Building. Fine. It's also *ugly*. Almost no one wants the World Trade Center to hog the glory, so guidebooks are apt to note that, with antenna, the

Empire State Building comes to 1,414 feet—considerably higher than the World Trade Center. The *World Almanac* does that.

But the World Trade Center has an antenna, too. If you count the antenna on the Empire State Building, you have to count the one on the World Trade Center. That increases the height of the World Trade Center to 1,710 feet, well above the Empire State Building.

On that antenna rests the World Trade Center's claim to being the tallest building, for the building proper was surpassed when Chicago's Sears Tower opened in 1973. The Sears Tower, of course, is usually considered the world's tallest building. The building proper is 92 feet taller than the World Trade Center, and 204 feet taller than the Empire State Building.

Despite its boxy shape, the Sears Tower is more flexible than the Empire State Building, swaying about six inches in high winds. The Sears Tower also has the slickest tour, complete with a talking model of the Sears Tower itself. As you circle the observation deck, the same voice of the Sears Tower explains such niceties as the "smart" wastebaskets (they melt to smother a fire automatically) and points out sights such as the Loop, Wrigley Field, and what the voice says is the most humane jail in the country, where every criminal has a five-inch window.

Neither the World Trade Center nor the Sears Tower is really the highest building, though. Once you start counting antennas, you have to count every antenna. Toronto's CN Tower is little more than an antenna, but it's much higher (1,821 feet) than any office building with or without antenna. It's a big tourist attraction in Toronto, as you can take an elevator into the CN Tower and enjoy a meal in the sybaritic Sky Pod restaurant. The restaurant (which revolves) is 1,140 feet up. That's high for a restaurant, although it is several hundred feet below the observation decks of the Sears Tower and the World Trade Center. Even in the upper, green-glass-enclosed deck of the Empire State Building you are higher than you can get in the CN Tower.

| | Stories | Height | With Antenna | Height of Observation Deck | No. of States Visible on a Clear Day |
|---|---|---|---|---|---|
| Warszawa Radio Tower | | 2,121 | 2,121 | | 0 |
| CN Tower | | 1,822 | 1,822 | 1,140 | 1* |
| Sears Tower | 110 | 1,454 | 1,707 | 1,353 | 4 |
| World Trade Center | 110 | 1,362 | 1,710 | 1,362 | 5 |
| Empire State Building | 102 | 1,250 | 1,414 | 1,050 | 5 |
| Tokyo Tower | | 1,093 | 1,093 | 820 | 0 |

*Plus one Canadian province, Ontario.

You could visit all these buildings and never learn that the *real* tallest building on earth is in Poland. It is the Warszawa Radio Tower in Konstantynow, Poland, which is just under 2,121 feet high. There is a catch: It's not self-supporting. The tower is held up with fifteen guy wires. Cut the wires and it will flop over. The Warszawa Tower is about as minimal as a 2,121-foot building can be. Made of tubular steel, it weighs only 615 tons (versus 145,000 tons for the CN Tower and 222,500 tons for the Sears Tower). There is no restaurant, no observation deck, no tour, no gift shop.

Does the Warszawa Radio Tower "count"? Sure it does. It is a building—it didn't grow there—and the top of it is farther off the ground than anything else built by man. The most you can say about the Sears Tower is that it is the tallest *office* building, exclusive of antenna.

THIRTEEN

# THE MOST
# COMPREHENSIVE
# ART MUSEUM

# TO THE AVERAGE

Joe, there are just seven famous paintings. They are Leonardo da Vinci's *Mona Lisa* and *The Last Supper,* Michelangelo's *The Creation of Adam,* James Whistler's *Arrangement in Grey and Black (Whistler's Mother),* Grant Wood's *American Gothic,* Thomas Gainsborough's *The Blue Boy,* and Salvador Dali's *The Persistence of Memory.* That this is an absurdly arbitrary list doesn't matter. These are the paintings that have become famous through crass reproductions and caricatures, through newspaper ads for car dealers and TV commercials for pudding.

Based on the average Joe's short list, the most complete museum was long the Louvre. It had two of the seven. For years the presence of the *Mona Lisa* and *Whistler's Mother* under one roof was a big part of the draw of this museum with American tourists, a fair proportion of whom would never go to a museum in their own town. Unfortunately, the same modernization drive that put public toilets in the Louvre also got *Whistler's Mother* transferred to the new Musée d'Orsay. The Musée d'Orsay is a separate building on the other side of the Seine, with a separate admission fee—in short, a completely different museum to the time-strapped tourist. Now no museum has more than one. To the well-traveled but undiscerning, the Louvre's distinction rests mainly on the fact that the *Mona Lisa* is the single most famous painting.

The renown of a work of art has to do with many things other than its merit. Works in big museums like the Louvre become better known than equally significant works in less accessible museums or private collections. It's self-perpetuating: Many of the famous paintings in the Louvre are famous in part because they're in the Louvre. Pundits occasionally argue that other museums, particularly Leningrad's cavernous Hermitage, are vastly underrated in popular estimation because they are less visited by Westerners.

For a quick but reasonably objective comparison of the world's major art museums, we consulted catalogues raisonnés (listings of all known works of a particular artist) of six Western artists. We tried to use the single most famous European painter of each century from the Renaissance to the present. Da Vinci represented the fifteenth century, Raphael the sixteenth, Rembrandt the seventeenth, Goya the eighteenth, van Gogh the nineteenth, and Picasso the twentieth. The list includes two Italians, two Dutchmen, and two Spaniards, of which one Dutchman and one Spaniard worked mostly in France. We tallied how many paintings (but not sculptures, drawings, or other works) of each of these artists there were in the world's principal museums of European art. For prolific

Picasso, many of whose paintings are unaccounted for, only his cubist period was used (as catalogued in Pierre Daix's *Picasso: The Cubist Years: A Catalogue Raisonné of the Paintings and Related Works*).

Raw numbers of paintings is admittedly a crude measure of the significance of a collection. The Prado's tiny collection of Picasso works, which includes *Guernica,* is more important than larger collections of lesser Picasso works elsewhere. Nevertheless, the numbers are a decent guide most of the time. Major museums attempt to maintain a level of quality in their collections, selling off lesser works to buy more important ones if necessary. A big museum with a dozen paintings of a particular artist can usually be counted upon to have truly significant paintings among them.

Two single-artist museums have extraordinary concentrations of works from the artists' estates. Amsterdam's van Gogh Museum has 104 of his paintings, and Paris's Picasso Museum has about 200 of his. Since we're interested in these artists only as they typify the distribution of paintings generally, these highly focused museums were not counted.

The major museum with the greatest holdings of the six tabulated artists is Madrid's Prado. It has 128 paintings, more than twice the total for any other museum. However, 118 of the 128 are works of Spain's own Francisco José de Goya. Had Gainsborough or Boucher been used to represent the eighteenth century, the Prado would not have been anywhere near number one.

If the Prado is discounted, the museum with the greatest number of tabulated paintings is the Hermitage. It has 58, and the Louvre has 40. (The Louvre would have had 61 counting a set of 21 van Goghs that were moved to the Musée d'Orsay.)

"Only the mice and I admire my treasures," boasted Catherine the Great, whose fabulous art collection in the Winter Palace became the nucleus of the Hermitage. For more than a century, the Hermitage was more a storehouse than an exhibition gallery. The Russian public clamored for the collection to be opened to public view, and a proper museum was opened in 1851. To show due respect, visitors were required to wear formal dress or uniform. The Hermitage now has more Rembrandts than the Louvre (21). It has strong holdings of Picasso (29), whose membership in the Communist Party popularized his art with the Soviets. Da Vinci, Raphael, and van Gogh are represented in the Hermitage; only Goya is missing. Nor are the holdings in these six tabulated artists unrepresentative. Their colleagues of equal and lesser fame are represented comparably well.

The Hermitage's paintings are not nearly as well known in the West as the Louvre's. Whether the Hermitage's best paintings are as choice as the Louvre's is a matter of opinion. You're comparing the tastes of the Russian rulers with the French. Both sent agents all over Europe with blank checks and instructions to buy the best. At times, both used force to get what money couldn't buy. Napoleon raided the art collections of conquered territories for the Louvre. Most of the works were later returned. The Hermitage's great art grab was for keeps. After the overthrow of the czars, the Bolsheviks stripped the mansions of the fled aristocracy. The Orwellian-sounding State Commission for the Registration of Works carefully catalogued the most significant private collections of art and shipped them to the Hermitage. In a few short years, the museum expanded to a degree probably not equaled anywhere else. The Hermitage continues to purchase works at a steady clip. All things considered, the wealth of significant European paintings at the Hermitage at least rivals and possibly exceeds the painting collection of the Louvre.

The Hermitage collection is broader-based than the Louvre's, too. The Hermitage has the world's second-best collection of French art; the Louvre does not have Russian art to speak of. In addition to European art, the Louvre has Classical, Egyptian, and Middle Eastern antiquities. So does the Hermitage, and its collection of classical antiquities is larger—the biggest outside of Greece and Italy. The Hermitage collects ancient and modern art of the Far East and has a token set of American works. Neither is represented at the Louvre.

| | Total paintings | Number of artists represented | Total percent of oeuvres | da Vinci | Raphael | Rembrandt | Goya | van Gogh | Picasso (Cubist) |
|---|---|---|---|---|---|---|---|---|---|
| Louvre, Paris | 40 | 4 | 39.4 | 8 | 13 | 14 | 5 | | |
| Prado, Madrid | 128 | 4 | 20.5 | | 8 | 1 | 118 | | 1 |
| National Gallery, London | 37 | 6 | 17.7 | 2 | 9 | 19 | 3 | 3 | 1 |
| Hermitage, Leningrad | 58 | 5 | 16.8 | 2 | 2 | 21 | | 4 | 29 |

| | Total paintings | Number of artists represented | Total percent of oeuvres | da Vinci | Raphael | Rembrandt | Goya | van Gogh | Picasso (Cubist) |
|---|---|---|---|---|---|---|---|---|---|
| Uffizi Gallery, Florence | 12 | 3 | 15.1 | 3 | 7 | 2 | | | |
| National Gallery, Washington, D.C. | 46 | 6 | 14.7 | 1 | 7 | 20 | 12 | 5 | 1 |
| Vatican Collections, Rome | 13 | 2 | 10.8 | 1 | 12 | | | | |
| Metropolitan Museum, New York | 48 | 5 | 9.5 | | 2 | 23 | 12 | 9 | 2 |
| Rijksmuseum, Amsterdam | 24 | 3 | 5.5 | | | 22 | 1 | 1 | |
| Art Institute, Chicago | 28 | 4 | 3.5 | | | 2 | 8 | 9 | 9 |
| Works accounted for, public and private collections worldwide: | | | | 29 | 164 | 422 | 772 | 879 | 893 |

Despite that, a case can be made that the Louvre has the more important collection. Rarity influences the significance of a work. Assume, for the sake of argument, that da Vinci and Picasso are artists of equal merit. You can see a Picasso practically anywhere. There are only a few places in the world you can see a da Vinci. It is reasonable to say that each da Vinci counts for more in a museum's collection.

The Louvre has 8 da Vincis out of about 29 known worldwide: more than a quarter of his entire oeuvre. In comparison, the

Hermitage's set of 29 cubist Picassos is only about 3 percent of the 893 known. Based on fraction of the artist's existing work housed there, the Louvre's da Vinci collection is more remarkable than the Hermitage's Picasso collection.

The Louvre has 27.6 percent of the world's da Vinci paintings, 7.9 percent of the Raphaels, 3.3 percent of the Rembrandts, and 0.6 percent of the Goyas. Add up these fractions for a total "score" of 39.4 percent. In other words, the tabulated holdings are the equivalent of 39 percent of the lifework of a painter in a class with da Vinci, Goya, or Picasso.

Doing the same thing for the Hermitage yields only 16.8 percent. The Russians took up collecting a little later than the French and got fewer of the rare artists of the Renaissance. When holdings are weighted for rarity like this, the Hermitage comes in fourth among major museums, after the Goya-laden Prado and the British National Gallery. This assessment is far from perfect—it probably gives too much weight to some minor da Vincis because of their extreme rarity—but the overwhelming lead of the Louvre shows that its collection is justly renowned.

While no American collection matches the great European galleries for quantity or rarity, the U.S. National Gallery in Washington has at least one painting by all six of the artists above. Only London's National Gallery matches that. New York's Metropolitan Museum, with its substantial collections of American, Asian, African, and Oceanic works, is probably the most cosmopolitan of the major collections—even more so than the Hermitage.

# FOURTEEN

# THE MOST COMPREHENSIVE ZOO

# THE BRONX ZOO

is the "largest zoo in America" according to Fred W. McDarrah in a 1978 guide, *Museums in New York*. It has a nice blend of naturalism and theme-park accouterments. You can't drive through, but you can buzz the animals on the monorail. It is also notable for a creepy set of moldering, child-oriented exhibits that once seemed neat. The Great Apes House dares you to face "the most dangerous animal in the world." It's a mirror—a gently misanthropic reminder not at all out of place in the Morris Park section of the Bronx. But is the Bronx Zoo really the best zoo? The San Diego Zoo gets a lot of publicity, and its T-shirts proclaim it the world's largest zoo. It may well be the richest. The San Diego Zoo's budget is the country's largest (about $28 million, vs. $20 million for the Bronx Zoo). That means fancy new digs for the animals every few years and amenities like the SkyFari Tram and the shroud of mist at the entrance to Tiger River. The zoo knows it's competing with jazzier attractions like Lion Country Safari, and compensates with better production values. A lazy man's favorite is Chicago's Lincoln Park Zoo. The nation's best-attended zoo, it is also one of the most compact. In winter a world-famed variety of species are conveniently packed chockablock into weatherproof compounds rather than spread out over a lot of habitat.

The simplest way of comparing zoo collections is by the number of animals (meaning individual animals, or "specimens" in zoo parlance). The biggest zoo by this measure is probably the Tama Zoo in Tokyo. It recently reported 27,631 specimens, compared with just 3,949 for the Bronx Zoo and 3,590 for the San Diego Zoo. The catch is that most of the Tama Zoo's specimens are *bugs*. Insects and other marginal life forms account for 25,983 of the total. Kids might get a brief rush out of an Insect House, but they're not going to stay there long. Half the time you look in the terrarium and don't even see anything. The bottom line is that the Tama Zoo has only 1,648 *real* animals with backbones. That's much fewer than the big American zoos have.

Counting each and every animal pads the totals of zoos with a lot of small creatures. The actual number of animals isn't that important, anyway. One coatimundi is as good as twenty. When you go to a zoo with persons of limited attention span, you want to be able to look at an animal and *move on to the next one fast.* Number of species is more the ticket.

The San Diego Zoo has about 767 species. That's the most in the United States. The Cincinnati Zoo is second with 736, and Bronx is third with 691. But the San Diego total is not even close to the world record. The *International Zoo Yearbook,* published by the London Zoological Society, is the standard reference on zoo animal populations, used when arranging breeding loans. According to data in the most recent edition (1987), the San Diego Zoo would be only eighth in the world in number of species. The West Berlin Zoo (Zoologischer Garten und Aquarium Berlin) is tops with 1,579 species, almost twice the number in the San Diego Zoo.

Northern Europe, particularly Germany and the Low Countries, is home to several renowned zoos. Both West Berlin and East Berlin have world-class zoos, and Antwerp, Amsterdam, and Rotterdam all have extraordinary zoos in a small geographic area.

The West Berlin Zoo, like many foreign zoos, doubles as an aquarium. It has hundreds of species of fish and invertebrates. The San Diego Zoo does not have fish, and in general, the U.S. civic pattern is to have a separate zoo and aquarium. Nor do most American zoos bother with insects, outside of a few proven crowd pleasers like the vinegar scorpion and tarantula.

It's not just how many species but which species. Some animals are more popular or rarer than others. A basic set of zoo animals would include the lion, tiger, elephant, giraffe, hippopotamus, zebra, and gorilla. A zoo lacking any of these seems incomplete. All except the tiger and gorilla are fairly common at major zoos.

We chose a list of 12 relatively rare but well-known and popular species from the *International Zoo Yearbook*'s 1985 census listing and tallied which of the largest zoos exhibited them. All 12 animals are either endangered in the wild or no longer exported from their native lands. The list includes the Galápagos tortoise, kiwi (any of the several species), koala, pygmy chimpanzee (the less common of the two species, cuter and smarter than the regular), gorilla, giant anteater, giant panda (despite its popularity, extremely rare in zoos), snow leopard, Przewalski's horse (the near-extinct ancestor of domestic horses), Indian rhinoceros, pygmy hippopotamus, and okapi. Animals listed as existing at an affiliated park (such as the San Diego Wild Animal Park and the London Zoo's Whipsnade) were credited to their main zoo as they are often on display there through rotations. Animals on breeding loan were credited to the zoo where they actually resided at the time of the census.

While the chart on page 221 is a rough index, the San Diego Zoo scored highest. It had 9 of the 12 animals—all except the Galápagos tortoise, kiwi, and giant panda. London was second with 8, and Antwerp tied with Los Angeles for third place. Though not the biggest, the San Diego Zoo probably has as many high-visibility animals as any zoo in the world.

| | Total | Galápagos Tortoise | Giant Anteater | Giant Panda | Gorilla var. | Indian Rhinoceros | Kiwi spp. | Koala | Okapi | Przewalski's Horse | Pygmy Chimpanzee | Pygmy Hippopotamus | Snow Leopard |
|---|---|---|---|---|---|---|---|---|---|---|---|---|---|
| San Diego | 9 | | x | | x | x | | x | x | x | x | x | x |
| London | 8 | | x | x | x | x | x | | x | x | | x | |
| Antwerp | 7 | | | | x | x | x | | x | x | x | x | |
| Los Angeles | 7 | | x | | x | x | x | x | | x | | | x |
| Chicago (Brookfield) | 6 | | x | | x | | x | | x | | | x | x |
| New York (Bronx) | 6 | | x | | x | x | | | | x | | x | x |
| East Berlin | 5 | x | | | x | x | | | | x | | x | |
| West Berlin | 5 | x | | x | | x | | | | x | | x | |
| Amsterdam | 4 | | | | x | x | | | | | | x | x |
| Cincinnati | 2 | | | | x | | | | | | | x | |
| Moscow | 2 | | | | | | | | | x | | | x |
| Sydney | 2 | | | | x | | | | | | | x | |

# THE BEST FISHING SPOT IN THE WORLD

# ALL FISHERMEN LIE.

This is the inescapable problem in comparing fishing spots. The fishing literature is rife with pronouncements about the best places to fish. "But what is the best fishing hole of all?" asks Ervin A. Bauer in *Travel/Holiday* (1979). "Where is that Promised Land which every fisherman, super-serious or otherwise, should sample some day? Where do the fish sometimes strike bare hooks? For *this* incurable angler at least, the answer is easy. It's southwestern Alaska."

"There are lots more fish here than anywhere else. Tons more," the *Los Angeles Times* quoted angler Pat Brian of Austin, Tex. (1988). He was talking about Los Cabos at the southern tip of the Baja peninsula. "We get three to four times more marlin per angler than they do in Hawaii," insisted Darrell Primrose, owner of a charter fleet in Cabo San Lucas, in the same article. Ads taken out by FONATUR, the Mexican tourist corporation that is developing the place, say Los Cabos has "the world's best marlin fishing . . . They say there are more marlin than people at Los Cabos." As the settlement of Cabo San Lucas has a permanent population of 900, "they" aren't necessarily saying that much.

Self-consistency is not high among the angler's virtues. In *Motor Boat and Sailing* (October 1987), Peter Wright asserts successively that St. Thomas, Virgin Islands, is "considered by many to be the top blue marlin spot in the Atlantic," but Abidjan, Ivory Coast, is "the premier blue marlin spot in the Atlantic," but "Cairns, Queensland, is the most consistent place in the world in yielding up large billfish."

Anecdotal evidence will settle nothing. A place that is very good in season is less good off season. Even in season, it may be lousy on a particular day. Opinions of globe-trotting anglers, while not to be ignored, are not always conclusive. No one has fished everywhere, for every species of game fish, in season and out, long enough to form an opinion not colored by a few days' run of luck.

Quality of fishing is not a constant. It is accepted that rod-and-reel fishing off American coasts is far poorer than it once was. Sailfish are not as abundant off Florida or Long Island. Marlin are less common off California. Although natural cycles may be a factor, there is little doubt that the overall decline of fishing in most of the industrialized world is largely due to commercial fishing. Tuna boats inevitably catch a lot of marlin and sailfish (along with the better-publicized dolphins). While they are required to release the marlin and sailfish, reports claim that about half are dead on release.

"The best fishing spot" is a self-defeating concept. If any place was all that good, everyone would go there, overfish it, and it wouldn't be so good. The fact remains that some place *is* the best (by whatever criteria) right now.

There are at least two ways of defining the best fishing spot. The most obvious conception is that it is the place where you are most likely to catch a fish. To put it another way, it's the place where you catch the most fish per hour, per day, or per week.

Not all fish are equal in the eyes of anglers. The coterie of accepted game fish (bass, trout, salmon, marlin, sailfish, tuna, tarpon, etc.) are prized more than other fish. Within any species, big fish are more prized than small fish. Many anglers would gladly trade any number of run-of-the mill specimens for one record breaker. The best fishing spot might be the place where you are most likely to catch a fish of record size.

Let's start with the second idea. The International Game Fish Association (IGFA) of Fort Lauderdale keeps size records on fish landed by rod and reel. They have been keeping saltwater records since 1939. In 1978, *Field & Stream* magazine donated their records on freshwater fish, dating from 1910. That makes the IGFA archive the most complete in the world.

IGFA reports are on the honor system. "Witnesses to the catch are highly desirable if at all possible," say the IGFA rules. That means you don't need witnesses. You do have to have a notary public (wow!) witness your signature on the report form. It is unlikely that any sportsman would have such bad form as to fabricate a catch out of whole cloth. They might fudge on technique. The IGFA has strict rules on how you can and can't catch a fish to qualify for a world record, and some think they err on the side of fastidiousness. Let anyone touch your rod or line while working the fish and you're out. Rod holders aren't allowed, nor is chumming. In order to establish a new weight record, you must catch a fish that is at least one-half of 1 percent heavier than the existing record. This conservative system keeps records on the books even if they've been narrowly bettered.

The 1989 edition of the IGFA's record book lists almost 400 all-tackle records for freshwater and saltwater fish. IGFA's size records are by no means randomly distributed. Part of the reason is geographic bias, and part is the real-world distribution of big fish. IGFA's records mostly document catches by Americans and Europeans, middle-class to wealthy people fishing for enjoyment. These fishermen favor certain areas (Long Island, Florida, the Caribbean, etc.). The more fishermen in a certain locale, the greater the chance that a record-breaking fish will be caught, provided such fish exist there in the first place.

There are thinly populated, rarely visited areas with a number of world records. That suggests that the largest fish are indeed concentrated in certain areas and that the IGFA records provide a rough idea of where these concentrations are.

We tallied the freshwater and saltwater records by state or province (United States, Canada, Australia, United Kingdom) and by nation, territory, island, or island group. Of the current size records for 121 of the most popular species of freshwater game fish, the largest concentration is in Alaska. It has seven world records (for Dolly Varden trout, inconnu, rainbow trout, and chinook, chum, pink, and sockeye salmon). That is significant in view of Alaska's small population.

This can be better appreciated by comparing the number of world records with the human population. Take all the states, nations, or territories with at least two records (a single record is too likely to be a fluke). Divide the number of records by the population of the region. The result, in descending number of record catches per population, is the following table:

**Fresh Water**

| | Records | Population (millions) | Records/ million |
|---|---|---|---|
| Northwest Territory (Canada) | 3 | 0.05 | 59.00 |
| Alaska | 7 | 0.53 | 13.00 |
| South Dakota | 3 | 0.71 | 4.20 |
| Manitoba | 2 | 1.07 | 1.90 |
| Tennessee | 5 | 4.80 | 1.04 |
| Georgia | 6 | 5.98 | 1.00 |
| Arizona | 3 | 3.32 | 0.90 |
| Mississippi | 2 | 2.63 | 0.76 |
| Alabama | 3 | 4.05 | 0.74 |
| British Columbia | 2 | 2.88 | 0.69 |
| Wisconsin | 3 | 4.79 | 0.63 |
| South Carolina | 2 | 3.38 | 0.59 |
| Sweden | 4 | 8.36 | 0.48 |
| Minnesota | 2 | 4.21 | 0.47 |
| Louisiana | 2 | 4.50 | 0.44 |
| Ontario | 4 | 9.02 | 0.44 |
| Florida | 5 | 11.68 | 0.43 |
| Indiana | 2 | 5.50 | 0.36 |
| Texas | 6 | 16.68 | 0.36 |
| North Carolina | 2 | 6.33 | 0.32 |

**Fresh Water**

|  | Records | Population (millions) | Records/ million |
|---|---|---|---|
| New York | 5 | 17.77 | 0.28 |
| Austria | 2 | 7.55 | 0.27 |
| Michigan | 2 | 9.15 | 0.22 |
| California | 5 | 26.98 | 0.19 |
| Pennsylvania | 2 | 11.89 | 0.17 |
| Colombia | 3 | 29.96 | 0.10 |
| Argentina | 2 | 31.19 | 0.06 |
| Brazil | 3 | 143.28 | 0.02 |

At the top of the list is Canada's Northwest Territories. Three records were set there, an amazing number given the scant resident population. In world records per million residents, the Northwest Territories rate about 59. That is many times more than any place else on the table. The Northwest Territories aren't much of a haven for visiting anglers either, at least not compared with places like Florida or even Alaska.

Alaska is second. Its seven records is the equivalent of 13 records per million residents. Compare this with Florida and California. Both have large populations. Dividing their record catches by the population shows that the number of records isn't so great in relative terms. Your chance of landing a record or near-record freshwater fish in Florida or California is probably a lot less than in Alaska.

Among the surprises are South Dakota and Manitoba, both of which are rated relatively good.

We can't really conclude that the Northwest Territories have the best freshwater fishing in the world. The records are concentrated in North America. The cluster of records in northern Canada and Alaska must have something to do with their being remote and little fished. If there is even better fishing somewhere more remote (Siberia? Patagonia?) but no one likely to report his catch to Fort Lauderdale goes there, the IGFA records cannot show it. That said, anyone aspiring to a record catch in North America would do well to try the subarctic rivers and lakes.

Doing the same thing for the IGFA records of 252 popular saltwater game fish produces this table:

**Salt Water**

|  | Records | Population (millions) | Records/ million |
|---|---|---|---|
| Christmas Island | 2 | 0.003 | 667.0 |
| Bermuda | 7 | 0.06 | 122.0 |
| Greenland | 3 | 0.05 | 57.0 |
| Northern Territory (Australia) | 2 | 0.14 | 14.0 |
| Azores | 3 | 0.29 | 10.0 |
| Alaska | 5 | 0.53 | 9.4 |
| Mauritania | 10 | 1.69 | 5.9 |
| Hawaii | 5 | 1.06 | 4.7 |
| Maine | 4 | 1.17 | 3.4 |

**Salt Water**

| | Records | Population (millions) | Records/ million |
|---|---|---|---|
| Florida | 39 | 11.68 | 3.34 |
| Fiji | 2 | 0.72 | 2.80 |
| Gambia | 2 | 0.77 | 2.58 |
| Canary Islands | 2 | 0.81 | 2.48 |
| Mauritius | 2 | 1.02 | 1.96 |
| New Hampshire | 2 | 1.03 | 1.95 |
| Costa Rica | 5 | 2.71 | 1.84 |
| New Zealand | 6 | 3.31 | 1.82 |
| Washington | 8 | 4.46 | 1.79 |
| Queensland | 4 | 2.51 | 1.60 |
| South Australia | 2 | 1.35 | 1.48 |
| Western Australia | 2 | 1.38 | 1.45 |
| Panama | 3 | 2.23 | 1.35 |
| Norway | 5 | 4.17 | 1.20 |
| New South Wales | 6 | 5.41 | 1.11 |
| North Carolina | 7 | 6.33 | 1.11 |
| Alabama | 3 | 4.05 | 0.74 |
| Sweden | 6 | 8.36 | 0.72 |
| Virginia | 4 | 5.79 | 0.69 |
| South Carolina | 2 | 3.38 | 0.59 |
| Ireland | 2 | 3.62 | 0.55 |
| New Jersey | 4 | 7.62 | 0.52 |
| Massachusetts | 3 | 5.83 | 0.51 |
| South Africa | 11 | 33.24 | 0.33 |
| Ecuador | 3 | 9.65 | 0.31 |
| Senegal | 2 | 6.98 | 0.29 |
| New York | 5 | 17.77 | 0.28 |

**Salt Water**

| | Records | Population (millions) | Records/ million |
|---|---|---|---|
| California | 6 | 26.98 | 0.22 |
| Mexico | 18 | 81.71 | 0.22 |
| England | 8 | 46.78 | 0.17 |
| Texas | 2 | 16.68 | 0.12 |
| Venezuela | 2 | 17.79 | 0.11 |
| Peru | 2 | 20.21 | 0.10 |
| Japan | 2 | 121.40 | 0.02 |

By far the most saltwater records (39) were set in Florida. That's kind of suspicious since the IGFA is based in Florida. Per population, Florida's share of the records is less remarkable—not quite as good as Maine. At that, Florida's angling population is boosted by out-of-state tourists.

Second in total number of records is Mexico. It's tough to evaluate the fishing in Mexico from this table. Mexico's large population drags down the records-per-million figure. However, most of the saltwater records were set off Baja California, which has a modest population. Judging from the surnames of the record holders, most or all were North American tourists. Considered separately, the Baja peninsula would probably rate near the top of the list.

Two places with notably strong showings are Mauritania (in western Africa) and Bermuda. They hold 10 and 7 records, respectively, so their high standing can hardly be an accident. Both are effectively points on the map, for Bermuda is the size of Manhattan, and all 10 of Mauritania's records come from the same place (Nouadhibou, a town at the northern end of the nation's coastline).

But none of these places comes anywhere close to Christmas Island. There are two Christmas Islands, one in the Pacific and one in the Indian Ocean. The one at the top of the list is the Pacific one. It is the site of two records (for longnose emperor and bluefin trevally). Two records is nothing to be dogmatic about, but it is suggestive. Since Christmas Island's resident population is only 3,000 people, it can claim almost 667 records per million population. That's five times what Bermuda has. Had Christmas Island just one record, it would rate higher than anyplace else listed above.

As with a lot of these places, the resident population is almost beside the point. Most of the records are set by tourists. If anything, this makes Christmas Island's standing all the more extraordinary. Bermuda attracts about 400,000 tourists a year, and many come to fish. At present, the only air service to Christmas Island is a weekly charter from Honolulu that can accommodate thirty-five but is often only half full. That means the annual number of Christmas Island tourists is somewhere around 1,000 (though *everyone* comes to fish). In record catches per tourist, Christmas Island would be over a hundred times better than Bermuda.

Among places presently frequented by North Americans, Christmas Island may be the best fishing spot by *quantity* of fish caught, too. Even as fish tales go, the stories about Christmas Island stand out. The usual assessment runs something like: "Take the best day you ever had and multiply it by three." Thirty catches an hour is claimed to be not unusual. Taking this with a grain of salt, it is apparent that the fishing is better than, say, around Miami.

Christmas Island is part of the nation of Kiribati, a confederation of atolls straddling the equator. It is 2,200 miles due south of Honolulu—about as remote from Hawaii as San Francisco is from New York. There is one hotel on the island. There is not much to do besides fish. Christmas Island was used for British nuclear tests from 1956 to 1962. Rumors of that having something to do with the fishing are doubtful. As far as the locals can remember, the fishing was always good. The world's largest atoll, Christmas Island is girt with coral shallows inches deep for miles out. The outsized lagoon is crammed with bonefish, barracuda, and assorted exotica: queenfish, ulua, and pupio. The bonefish grow to record size. Although the IGFA bonefish world record of 19 pounds (set in 1962 off Zululand, South Africa) has yet to be broken, Christmas Island guide "Big Eddie" Corrie claims to have seen a bonefish in a net that weighed 23 pounds. (Net catches don't count for IGFA records.)

Not only are the fish numerous; they are unafraid of man. Christmas Island was uninhabited when Captain James Cook discovered it on Christmas Eve 1777. The island's Polynesian residents are recent transplants. There still aren't many fishermen. Bonefish is not very good to eat; it's illegal for nonresidents to keep their catch anyway. In recent years Kiribati has allowed the Soviet Union unlimited commercial fishing rights. In the long run, that can't help the fishing. For now, almost everyone who goes to Christmas Island comes back saying it's the best fishing spot anywhere.

There are a lot of little dots on the map of the Pacific. Just because Christmas Island is good doesn't mean it is the best in the entire world. Corrie, the Christmas Island guide, claims that there is better fishing off Canton Island, and better fishing yet off Fanning Island. And he's in a better position to know than we are. Canton Island is an almost deserted atoll several hundred miles to the west of Christmas Island. Fanning is the island to the north of Christmas, smaller but more lush because of greater rainfall. Corrie says the fish there are even less afraid of man, for there aren't *any* fishermen. Reason suggests that any number of uninhabited atolls with large shallow lagoons are at least the equal of Christmas Island in fishing.

# THE MOST DIFFICULT MOUNTAIN- EERING PEAK

# UNCLIMBED MOUNTAINS

are vanishing quickly. There are 14 "eight-thousanders"—peaks of greater than 8,000 meters (26,247 feet). Not one had been climbed as recently as 1950. Now *all* have. There are over 300 seven-thousanders (at least 22,966 feet high). The seven-thousanders were passed over in the race for Everest and its glamorous neighbors. They just weren't worth bothering with. Then, in the 1960s and 1970s, after eight-thousanders had been taken, the seven-thousanders started to look good. Whatever else makes a person climb a mountain, ego is one reason, and it sounds better to be the first to scale some mountain rather than the 27th to ascend Everest or K2. By the end of the 1970s, the seven-thousanders were gone.*

* These figures, long accepted by climbers, may be wrong. In 1987 satellite measurements established the height of K2 as 29,064 feet. That is higher than the long-accepted height of Mount Everest, but the measurements indicated that Everest is about 800 feet higher than K2. Everest would then be about 29,864 feet high. If the heights of Himalayan peaks have been

The highest unclimbed peaks are in Nepal. There are still six-thousanders left there. The government forbids climbing except on certain peaks, and many six-thousanders are out of bounds. If and when Nepal eases the climbing regulations, there will be a near-frenzy to get permission. Quite irreversibly, the sense of adventure is being depleted from the sport.

Since all the highest peaks have been climbed, it is possible to speak with some confidence about their relative degrees of challenge. It is clear that the height of a mountain may have relatively little to do with its difficulty. This paradox has long fueled debate among climbers and would-be climbers.

Everest is not the most difficult mountain to climb. If by "most difficult" you mean the mountain whose summit is hardest to attain *by any route,* then it is probably K2. K2 or Godwin Austen, (probably) the second-highest peak in the world, is in Kashmir about 800 miles northwest of Everest.

Different approaches to a summit have different degrees of difficulty. Climbers often regard different routes as distinct challenges. Today there is no mountain so high it cannot be climbed at all. There are routes that are yet unconquered.

Among such routes, the one with the most failed attempts by world-class climbers might fairly be called the most difficult. By this criterion, the hardest mountaineering challenge would probably be the famous south face of Lhotse I. Reinhold Messner understatedly called it the "last great Himalayan problem."

Lhotse is a set of three Himalayan summits on the Nepal-Tibet border. It is south of Everest and joined to it by a 25,000-

---

underestimated, there may be a few more eight-thousanders and seven-thousanders than thought.

foot ridge. Lhotse I, the fourth-highest mountain in the world at 27,939 feet (by the old figures), was climbed by a Swiss team in 1956. It has long been appreciated that the south face presents unique challenges. Among them is an incredible 10,000-foot vertical drop, of which 1,000 feet is *overhanging.*

Theoretically, it could be done with modern techniques. A lot of climbers thought their chances were good enough to try. A Japanese team started up and turned back in 1973. An Italian team lead by Messner and Riccardo Cassin were foiled by avalanches at the 24,600-foot level in 1975. More avalanches took out a 1976 Japanese expedition. In 1980 Nicolas Jaeger of France set out solo and was never seen again. In 1981 a veritable mob of twenty-seven Yugoslav climbers attacked the south face and were driven back a mere 500 feet from the summit by a death-dealing storm. They had spent 63 days on the mountain, dodging avalanches and rockfalls on 59 of them. In 1986 a ten-man Spanish team called off their attempt when one climber fell 2,400 meters (a mile and a half!). The team doctor descended to recover the body and got severe frostbite in nine fingers. The fallen man's body was never found. Another 1986 attempt turned back 350 meters from the summit. That makes the record zero successes out of seven recent, sophisticated attempts.

Mountain climbing is a test of endurance, planning, and adaptation to altitude. Much of what makes a mountain difficult to climb has little to do with altitude, though. A vertical face poses a certain type of problem whether it is on a Himalayan peak or a minor crag in the Adirondacks. Climber John Harlan

III rated the Salathe Wall of Yosemite's El Capitan as "the finest rock climb in the world" in his *The Climber's Guide to North America*. El Capitan is scenic, but it's only about 5,000 feet above the valley.

On a foot-by-foot basis, the hardest climbs are not necessarily on tall mountains. The Yosemite Decimal System rates the difficulty of climbs across rock independently of altitude. It pertains to specific routes and is based on the hairiest part of a climb. (If a climb is mostly easy but requires a difficult maneuver at one point, that difficult maneuver is going to be the bottleneck.)

The rating consists of a decimal number like 5.3. The number to the left of the decimal point is a general rating:

| First Number | |
|---|---|
| 1 | Trail hiking |
| 2 | Rough hiking |
| 3 | Rock scrambling |
| 4 | Moderately difficult climbing; most climbers use ropes |
| 5 | Most difficult free climbing |
| 6 | Artificial climbing |

Class 1 designates a hike. Class 2 is a rougher hike, with some use of hands for balance. Class 3 embraces the easiest true climbs. Class 3 terrain is steep enough so that you use your hands more or less constantly. Inexperienced climbers may want to use ropes. Class 4 is difficult enough so that most climbers use ropes.

The hardest *free* climbs are in class 5. Free climbing is using hands and feet on natural holds in the rock itself: ledges, hollows, and cracks. Class 6 is for climbs that would be humanly impossible save for artificial hand- and footholds such as bolts. It is possible to climb even a sheer wall of rock by placing bolts into the rock and using them to work your way up. Many climbers feel that placing bolts for climbing is no different from building an escalator up the side of the mountain. It just isn't sporting. "Today's climber carries his courage in his rucksack," Reinhold Messner complained in 1969, when artificial climbing was more prevalent than now. He felt that it had led to a "murder of the impossible."

Classes are subdivided with numbers to the right of the decimal point. Originally there was a single digit, from 0 to 9, in order of increasing difficulty. Climbs that were believed to be the absolute limit of human free-climbing ability were 5.9.

With the escalating level of skill and determination, climbers eventually scaled routes significantly more difficult than those that had been rated 5.9. Rather than downgrade previous ratings, they added a 5.10 rating (a "five point ten," not the same as a 5.1). This designated climbs a notch harder than the 5.9 climbs, even though they were done without aid. As ever harder climbs were bagged, they added a 5.11, 5.12, 5.13, and—the limit for the time being—5.14. Yosemite's Salathe Wall is rated 5.12.

Some climbers create even finer distinctions with letter suffixes. Each decimal class such as 5.10 may be divided into four subclasses, 5.10a, 5.10b, 5.10c, and 5.10d, from easiest to hardest. Under this system, 5.11a comes after 5.10d.

At the more rarefied levels of skill, the determining factor is neither altitude nor verticality. It is the size and position of hand- and footholds. The natural holds are mostly cracks in the rock face. Climbers ascend by forcing hands and feet tightly into the cracks. The difficulty of using a crack depends on its width. Climbers recognize "finger cracks," "hand cracks," "fist cracks," "foot cracks," and "body cracks." A crack too small to get a finger in it is useless, as is one so wide that it cannot be bridged by the arms and legs. Some of the most difficult climbs follow an "off-width" crack. This is one too wide to secure a fist but too narrow for the whole body. There are ways of dealing with off-width cracks, but all are strenuous and painful.

You can't gauge the precise size of cracks from the ground or a topographic map. It is therefore impossible to say how difficult a route is until someone has climbed it, and only routes that have been climbed have a Yosemite Decimal System number.

The climbs rated 5.14 are the most difficult climbs anyone has accomplished without artificial aid. Smith Rock, a series of towers and cliffs in an arid part of Oregon, has a climb called "To Bolt or Not to Be" that is rated 5.14b. It is on a cliff called the Dihedrals and was first climbed by J. B. Tribout in 1986. This is, at the moment, the most difficult successfully completed climb in North America. (There are also some 5.14s in Europe.) It's not, of course, the hardest climb of all. There are harder climbs that are rated 6 or are unrated. Some of the climbs now rated 6 will doubtless be free-climbed someday and receive a rating like 5.15.

Oddly enough, there is a mere 12-foot-high *rock* that has never been climbed. It is called Milton. It is in Eldorado Springs, Colo. There are many tempting rock climbs of 20 or 30 feet that have foiled all challengers, but Milton seems to be the shortest undefeated climb. In defeated world-class climbers per foot, it is a good candidate for the hardest climb of all.

Rock climbers have scaled the easier sides of Milton. Literally thousands of attempts to scramble up its southeast side have all failed. Milton is near the International Alpine School, so it has been the subject of an incredible amount of sophisticated analyses, trials, and postmortem analyses, all of which have proven futile. Climbers like Charlie Fowler, Bob Candelaria, and David Breashears have swarmed to Milton like moths to a flame. These are not the sort of guys who try something once and give up. Each has tried Milton many, many times. Each has failed every single time.

Milton doesn't look all that hard to climb. It is made out of ordinary sandstone. There are deceptively generous foot- and handholds. The trouble is, they are placed in just such a way as to prevent a being of humanoid proportions from using them. The best anyone has ever done is about 4 feet off the ground.

# SEVENTEEN

# THE MOST PROFITABLE PROPERTY IN MONOPOLY

# WHAT IS

the best property to buy in Monopoly? Many players are sure it's the classy Blue color group, Boardwalk and Park Place. Others are sure it's the low-rent Purple district, Mediterranean and Baltic avenues. Still others think it makes no difference which properties you buy.

Yet some Monopoly properties are significantly better than others. The rents are *not* in direct proportion to costs of properties, houses, and hotels, and this makes a big difference.

Take the amount of rent you collect when someone lands on a property and divide that by the cost of the property. That's the return on investment. For cheapie Mediterranean Avenue, that's a $2 rent divided by a $60 cost, or a 3.33 percent return every time someone lands on the property.

Of course, the idea is to build houses and hotels so you can charge higher rents. To do that, you have to own all the properties of a particular color. One reason for the popularity of the

Purple and Blue color groups is that they have just two properties rather than the usual three. It is easier to complete these color groups. Once you have all the properties in a color group, the rent is doubled, even without adding any houses. This doubles the return on investment for each property.

To figure the return for improved property, you have to take into account the cost of the houses or hotels. Adding a house on Mediterranean Avenue costs $50. This combined with the property cost of $60 makes a total cost of $110. With one house, the rent is raised to $10. The return is then $10/$110 or 9.09 percent.

The utilities and railroads work a little differently. Each of the four railroads has a rent of $25 that doubles with each additional railroad owned, but no houses or hotels may be added. When you own one utility, the rent is four times whatever the person landing on it rolled with the dice. Since the average total of two standard dice is 7, the rent amounts to 4 times 7 dollars, or $28, in the long run. When both utilities are owned, the rent is raised to ten times the dice amount—an average of $70. Dividing these by the cost ($150) gives the return on investment.

Okay. Of all the properties on the board, the ones with the best return on investment in their unimproved state are—surprisingly—the two utilities, the Electric Company and the Water Works. The average rent of $28 amounts to a return of 18.7 percent. Next best, but far behind, are the four railroads and the Boardwalk. Each has a return of 12.5 percent. In general, the return on the regular properties increases counterclockwise from Go, with a few anomalies.

The next phase of the game is acquiring a complete property

group. This doubles the returns on the regular properties, more than doubles the return on the utilities, and increases the railroads' return by a factor of eight. When you have all four railroads, you can charge a rent of $200, which is what each cost in the first place—a 100 percent return on investment.

There are four railroads, making it more difficult to acquire the lot than to acquire the three ordinary properties. But even if you have just three railroads (for a rent of $100), the return is 50 percent. That is still greater than any other complete set of properties. At this stage of the game, the railroads are the best deal.

You can't add houses to railroads, though. Since improvements to regular properties require ownership of entire color groups, it makes sense to calculate returns for groups rather than for individual properties. Suppose you add one house to each property in each color group. The highest return on investment is the Blue group, Boardwalk and Park Place, with an average return of 32.6 percent. (This is calculated as the *average* of the Blue's rents with one house, divided by the *average* property cost plus the cost of one house.) This return is still far less than the railroads' 100 percent, or the utilities' 46.7 percent, even without houses.

Figuring the returns for all the properties at all levels of improvement gives us this handy table:

|  | Unim-proved | Color Group | 1 House | 2 Houses | 3 Houses | 4 Houses | Hotel | Average Return |
|---|---|---|---|---|---|---|---|---|
| Purple | 5.0% | 10.0% | 13.6% | 28.1% | 64.3% | 92.3% | 112.9% | 46.6% |
| Light Blue | 6.2% | 12.4% | 21.2% | 45.2% | 109.0% | 135.8% | 158.8% | 69.80% |
| Violet | 7.3% | 14.5% | 21.6% | 46.1% | 104.4% | 118.8% | 123.6% | 62.32% |
| Orange | 7.9% | 15.7% | 25.6% | 53.4% | 116.4% | 130.7% | 140.8% | 70.05% |
| Red | 8.2% | 16.5% | 24.8% | 50.6% | 105.9% | 107.8% | 109.2% | 60.42% |
| Yellow | 8.5% | 17.0% | 27.2% | 60.0% | 113.9% | 114.4% | 114.7% | 65.11% |
| Green | 8.7% | 17.4% | 26.9% | 58.0% | 102.9% | 102.4% | 100.7% | 59.58% |
| Blue | 11.3% | 22.5% | 32.6% | 70.8% | 127.9% | 127.4% | 127.0% | 74.20% |
| Utilities | 18.7% | 46.7% |  |  |  |  |  | 42.67% |
| Railroads | 12.5% | 100.0% |  |  |  |  |  | 87.50% |

No regular property does as well as the railroads until improved to three houses. Then all the color groups except Purples do slightly better than the railroads. The most profitable is still the Blues (127.9 percent). Second most profitable is not the Greens, as you might think, but the Oranges (116.4 percent).

With four houses or a hotel, the Blues actually sag a little. Their return dips to 127.4 percent for four houses, and 127.0 percent for hotels. This doesn't mean you shouldn't put hotels on Boardwalk and Park Place, but only that the high price of houses/hotels there ($200) does not raise the rent enough to boost the return on investment. The most profitable properties when highly improved are the Light Blues—Oriental, Vermont, and Connecticut avenues. With hotels, this group offers the best return in the game, 158.8 percent. Having someone land on these properties just twice more than pays for the cost of all three properties and the hotels on them.

The last column gives the return averaged over all levels of improvement—an overall indication of how desirable the properties are. Railroads come out best; the Blues are the best improvable properties.

That doesn't settle the argument, though. Not every property is equally likely to be landed upon and produce a rent.

Some Chance and Community Chest cards send players directly to certain properties. There is not a card for *every* property, so the net effect is by no means uniform. There are Chance cards that send you to St. Charles Place, Illinois Avenue, the Boardwalk, the Reading Railroad, the nearest railroad (two cards), and the nearest utility. The nearest-utility card directs the player to pay the owner ten times the amount on the dice (a higher than usual rent if the owner only has the one utility), and the nearest-railroad card specifies twice the normal rent.

Even cards that seem to be neutral subtly favor certain properties. There is a Chance card that tells you to go back three spaces. There are only three Chance squares, and they don't move around. On one, the card sends you to Income Tax; on another, to a Community Chest, and on another, to New York Avenue.

Also, rolls of the dice favor some properties. To see how, note that various game situations move players to the Go or the Jail square. The game starts at Go; two Chance and Community

Chest cards send players to Go; a Chance card, the "Go to Jail" square, and the rule about rolling three doubles send players to Jail. On the player's next turn (or when the player gets out of Jail), the squares corresponding to likely rolls of the dice are favored.

It's impossible to roll a one with two dice, so Mediterranean (the space after Go) and St. Charles Place (the space after Jail) get skipped over. The most common roll with two standard dice is a seven. A Chance square is seven spaces after Go, and a Community Chest is seven after Jail. This apparently was intentional, to prevent a property from being landed on too frequently. However, the second most common rolls of the dice, sixes and eights, put the player on properties—Oriental or Vermont for players on Go and St. James or Tennessee for players in Jail.

Of the color groups, the Purples and the Greens are stiffed by the Chance and Community Chest cards and by the Go and Jail squares. Every other group has at least one card or likely roll going for it. Most favored are the Oranges, since they are a likely roll for a player getting out of Jail, and, furthermore, the "Go Back Three Spaces" card sends players to New York Avenue one out of three times.

But are the Oranges favored enough to beat out the Light Blues? To settle this, we rolled dice repeatedly and moved game pieces around the board as in a real game. Card instructions, rules about going to Jail, and so forth were implemented normally. (It was assumed that players landing in Jail would pay the fine to get out on their next turn.) We kept track of how frequently game pieces landed on each square, and averaged the results for each color group.

Since an average roll is 7, a player has about a one in seven chance of landing on any particular property during each circuit of the board. The Oranges, which were indeed the most favored, stood an average 17 percent chance per square per circuit of the board. The least-landed-upon groups were the utilities (11 percent each) and then the Purples (12 percent each).

This experiment pointed up a significant nonobvious fact about the game: the surprising importance of the "Go to Jail" square. Far more players are sent to Jail than to Go or any square specified by the Chance or Community Chest cards. The "Go to Jail" square snares about one in seven players approaching it. That means the two sides of the board between Jail and "Go to Jail" are frequently repeated on a circuit. The Jail traffic is a windfall. Players that would have landed on the Greens or Blues on their next move land on the Violets or Oranges instead.

Most favored are the Oranges. The Electric Company is reachable from Jail, though it requires snake eyes, a long shot. State and Virginia avenues (Purple) and the Pennsylvania Railroad are more likely rolls. All the Orange properties are favored, particularly St. James (6 from Jail) and Tennessee (8th after Jail), either of which can be rolled in doubles, one way of getting out of Jail. The Oranges, as well as the Reds and Yellows, may also be reached in more than one roll from Jail.

The real story is the weighted return on investment. Multiply the average return on investment by the chance of landing on the color group. The result takes into account not only how high the rent is but how likely one is to collect it. This, finally, is what we want. The revised table goes:

| | Average Return on Investment | Average Chance of Landing on Property in Group (Per Circuit of Board) | Return per Circuit of Board |
|---|---|---|---|
| Railroads | 87.5% | 16% | 14.0% |
| Orange | 70.1% | 17% | 11.7% |
| Blue | 74.2% | 14% | 10.0% |
| Red | 60.4% | 16% | 9.87% |
| Yellow | 65.1% | 15% | 9.77% |
| Light Blue | 69.8% | 13% | 9.07% |
| Violet | 62.3% | 14% | 8.93% |
| Green | 59.6% | 15% | 8.74% |
| Purple | 46.6% | 12% | 5.59% |
| Utilities | 42.7% | 11% | 4.55% |

*The conventional Monopoly wisdom is wrong.* The most profitable group all around is the railroads. Each time an opponent passes Go, each railroad is likely to earn back about 14 percent of the money invested in it.

The utilities are the *worst* properties. The high rents for single utilities are a sop to make up for the fact that few players land on them.

The best group you can build houses on is the Oranges, better than the Light Blues thanks to the Jail traffic. The Boardwalk and Park Place aren't as preeminent as many think, and the Purple color group has the worst return of improvable properties—players overshoot them.

However, you can't plan on buying the Oranges or Railroads and pass up chances to buy other properties. Champions in Monopoly tournaments agree that the proper strategy is to buy everything you land on *unless* two of the three properties are already owned by two different players.

# EIGHTEEN

# THE HIGHEST-SCORING WORD IN SCRABBLE

# WHAT CHILLS

enthusiasm for the game of Scrabble is that the highest-scoring words tend to be deviant yet tolerated spellings of words that are obscure to begin with. Just check the *Official Scrabble Dictionary.* An unconscionable share of highest-scoring words are variants of two words *guaranteed not to enter non-Scrabble conversation:* ZINCKY and KOLKHOZ.

Forewarned is forearmed. What is the highest-scoring legitimate word in Scrabble, according to the *Official Scrabble Dictionary?*

The high-scoring letters are Z and Q (10 points each) and J and X (8 points each). Clearly, the best you can do with a two-letter word is 9 points: AX and OX or, more esoteric, JO (sweetheart, mostly Scottish) and XI (the Greek letter or subatomic particle).

The best three-letter word is ZAX (19 points). That's a tool for cutting roof slates. It's such a good word that you can't beat its plural, ZAXES, among the five-letter words.

Conventional wisdom correctly rates QUIZ as the highest-scoring four-letter word (22 points). Its combination of two 10-point letters is so good that no five-letter word matches it. (Plurals and suffixes take you into seven letters.) JAZZ would score 29 points *if* there were two Z tiles. As it is, you have to use one of the blank tiles, which doesn't give you any points. That gives a score of only 19.

The best *real* five-letter word is probably ZIPPY (21 points). The *Official Scrabble Dictionary* also lists ZINKY (real challenge bait this: "containing or having the appearance of zinc" —you know, one of those words you save up to spring when the right situation comes up). At that, *zinky* is usually spelled *zincky;* it is only a recognized variant. The aforementioned ZAXES is worth 21 points as well.

The highest-scoring six-letter word the average person would recognize is KIBITZ (21 points). Better is KOLHOZ (22), a less common spelling of *kolkhoz,* a Soviet agricultural collective. It's in the *Official Scrabble Dictionary,* but almost any regular dictionary will just have KOLKHOZ, and try explaining that to your opponents. The highest-scoring six-letter words are ZINCKY, the preferred version of ZINKY, and QUEZAL, a begrudgingly permitted spelling of QUETZAL. Both rate 24 points.

QUETZAL, BAZOOKA, JONQUIL, and QUIXOTE are often mentioned as superior seven-letter words. Just as good are some variants of QUIZ, the best being QUIZZED. This requires a blank tile for the second Z and thus scores 25 points rather than the theoretical 35. The same goes for JAZZMAN and the fantastic-looking ZYZZYVA (a weevil genus that some consider a common name; famous as the last word in many dictionaries). A possible Scrabble word, ZYZZYVA requires the Z tile, the V tile, both Y tiles, and both blank tiles. The theoretical score of 43 is reduced to 23 by the blanks. The best seven-letter words are BEZIQUE (a pinochle-like card game played with a deck of 64 cards), and CAZIQUE (a bird): 27 points each.

The best eight-letter word is ZWIEBACK (28 points)—a nice, noncontroversial word that people have heard of. It's not a trademark.

Bonus squares add another level of subtlety. The best you can do with a two-letter word is to place it on one of the red triple-word-score squares for 3 times 9 points: 27 points. No other bonuses can apply. Ditto for three-letter words: Getting ZAK on a red square gives you 3 times 19 or 57 points.

Two bonuses are possible with a four-letter word. Inspection of the board layout shows that the best possible configuration is a word that spans a red triple-word square and a light blue double-letter square. The double-letter bonus necessarily applies to the first or last letter in the word. That's no problem because QUIZ has its valuable letters on either end. It could be worth 22 plus 10, the sum times three: 96 points.

It's also possible for a five-, six-, or seven-letter word to span triple-word and double-letter bonuses. In the most advantageous position, ZAXES, ZINKY, or ZIPPY would be worth 93 points. QUEZAL or ZINCKY could score 102, and BEZIQUE or CAZIQUE could rate 111.

That's not nearly as good as you can do. The ultimate grand slam of Scrabble is having ZWIEBACK straddle two triple-word squares. Then (check rule No. 13) the score is *nine times* the raw value for the word.

All the triple-word bonus squares are on the outer edge of the board, exactly seven squares apart. The Z would have to go on one triple-word square, and the K on the other. Either the E or the B would fall on a double-letter square. The B would be most advantageous. In that case you would have 28 points for ZWIE-BACK plus an extra 3 points for the doubled B, the sum times nine: 279 points. That exceeds the points scored in many entire games.

There's no point in arguing if ZWIEBACKS is an acceptable plural. To make it, you would have to have the E rather than the B fall on the double-letter square. That would result in a lower score, even with the extra letter: 261.

# NINETEEN

# THE
# HARDEST
# CROSSWORD
# PUZZLE

# THE NEW YORK TIMES'S

crossword puzzle, under the editorship of Eugene T. Maleska, is one of the most enjoyable of newspaper crosswords. A literate reader has a fair shot at completing it. The end game is riveting. Difficult clues are solved by cross-solution and revealed to be delightfully off-base. Few crosswords are as funny as the *New York Times*'s often is.

Many puzzle fans argue, rightly or not, that the *New York Times* puzzle is the hardest of traditional American-style puzzles. Some say other puzzles are the hardest. A 1988 Associated Press story cited unnamed "puzzle experts" as maintaining that "the most challenging puzzles can be found in *Games* magazine, the Dell 'Champion' series, and the Sunday puzzles of *Newsday, The San Francisco Examiner, The Boston Globe, The Washington Post* and *The New York Times.*"

The hardest crossword puzzle is not necessarily the most fun to work. Nor, looking at it from the other side of the table, is it necessarily harder to construct a hard puzzle than an easy one.

It's no trick to construct a brain buster out of all those obscure little words in crossword puzzle dictionaries. A point of contention with puzzle editors and solvers is "double-blinding"—having two hopelessly obscure words intersect. You have a clue like "Indonesian ox" crossing "Laborer (archaic)" and leaving an unfillable gap. This certainly makes the puzzle difficult. Maleska intentionally double-blinds; other editors think it anathema. Most solvers aren't crazy about it.

There's a distinction to completing a hard puzzle. It's not a distinction that counts for much in the real world, but it's a distinction nonetheless. Are Sunday puzzles really harder than the weekday puzzles? Are the aforementioned puzzles really the hardest? To allow direct comparison, we assembled a group of volunteers and had them work sample puzzles from newspapers and magazines.

Each person worked on photocopies of puzzles clipped from over two dozen newspapers and magazines. Since many of the bigger papers' puzzles are syndicated to other papers, this sample included most of the puzzle features Americans work on a given day. The solvers worked without reference books or any outside help until deadlocked—until they would normally call it quits. They were allowed to guess where uncertain. Then the number of correctly filled-in words was determined from the published solution and divided by the total number of clues. The resulting completion rate was averaged among all the participants for each puzzle.

The skills of the solvers varied. Some were avid crossword fans, and some had not done a crossword in years. Since each panelist worked each puzzle, the completion rates indicate relative difficulty.

Most newspaper puzzles are constructed by free-lancers and are not of identical difficulty from one day to the next. Except as mentioned, our test used only one specific puzzle for each feature, and thus is an exact guide of difficulty only for that day. Most puzzle editors, however, try to keep difficulty fairly constant.

Several puzzles were so easy that most panelists completed them without a hitch. The child-like puzzles in the *San Francisco Chronicle* and *St. Louis Post-Dispatch* each allowed a 100 percent completion rate. The latter is only a 13 by 13 grid. (The St. Louis paper also carries the *New York Times* puzzle.) Subjectively, the easiest puzzle of all was the *Highlights for Children*-esque number in the *Dallas Morning News.* "Acorn tree" (three letters). "Twelvemonth" (four letters). Hmm . . .

*New York* magazine's puzzle deserves special mention. Widely appreciated as one of the better puzzles, it scored very easy in our test. Many of our workers completed every clue correctly. Everyone agreed that it was a good puzzle, though. It took both time and thought to solve. Most of the other puzzles with near-total completion rates were the sort where you could fill a good deal of it in on the first pass. With the *New York* puzzle, clues became apparent only gradually. It didn't rely on obsolescent terms and double-blinding.

Among the puzzles with completion rates in the 90s are those of the *Chicago Tribune* (97 percent), the *Washington Post* (94 percent), and the *Boston Globe* (91 percent). All these puzzles were easier than the one in *TV Guide* (90 percent). The completion rates for the latter were skewed according to solvers' TV viewing habits. For couch potatoes, it's almost pointless. You don't need the "down" clues.

*Games* magazine offers a variety of puzzles at different levels of difficulty. The editors rate its puzzles with stars, one being easy and three being hard. We tried one of their "two-star" puzzles and found it a cinch, the completion rate being 95 percent.

The puzzles in the *New York Times, USA Today,* and the *Los Angeles Times* scored so close to each other that they are best considered to be of roughly equal difficulty. Our group achieved a 77 percent completion rate with the daily *New York Times* puzzle. ("I get too many letters from fans that say the puzzles aren't hard enough," Maleska once said when asked why he didn't make the puzzles easier.) We found no indication that the Sunday puzzle (in *The New York Times Magazine)* is any harder. It's just bigger (21 by 21 cells vs. 17 by 17). It takes more time to solve, of course, but the average clue did not appear to be more difficult. The completion rate on the Sunday puzzle was 86 percent.

Maleska also moonlights for *Dell Crossword Puzzles.* (The mark of the hard-core puzzler is going out and buying this magazine.) Dell's puzzles are rated easy, medium, hard, expert, and challenger. We used a challenger puzzle created by (not just edited by) Maleska. "Here's a real toughie for you," Maleska warned. Despite that, it was almost exactly as difficult as the *New York Times* puzzle.

Both *USA Today*'s and the *Los Angeles Times*'s puzzles were heavy on gratuitously obscure terms that scarcely exist outside of a crossword dictionary. That's not as satisfying as a puzzle that manages to define better-known words in oblique ways. Much of the time, the *Los Angeles Times*'s puzzle is notable for deceptive and multiply ambiguous clues. On the first pass, "amusingly outlandish" (five letters) sounds so much like "droll" you might be tempted to fill it in even without checking the intersecting clues. Then you find that there's an M in the middle: "comic"? The correct word was "campy."

The putative intellectual level of the publication is not always reflected in its crossword. If anything, there may be an element of overcompensation, with less prestigious papers favoring super-hard crosswords. The *Denver Post* and *Dallas Times Herald* carry the King Features Syndicate puzzle (credited to Eugene Sheffer). This was much harder than the *New York Times* puzzle and was the toughest tested: 63 percent.

| **American-Style Puzzles** | | **Clues Solved** |
|---|---|---|
| Daily | *Denver Post* (King Features) | 63% |
| Daily | *Los Angeles Times* | 75% |
| Daily | *USA Today* | 76% |
| Daily | *New York Times* | 77% |
| Monthly | *Dell Crossword Puzzles* magazine (challenger) | 78% |
| Daily | *New York Daily News* | 82% |
| Daily | *Miami Herald* | 85% |
| Sunday | *New York Times* | 86% |
| Sunday | *San Francisco Examiner* | 86% |
| Weekly | *TV Guide* magazine | 90% |
| Daily | *Boston Globe* | 91% |
| Daily | *Atlanta Journal & Constitution* | 94% |
| Daily | *Washington Post* | 94% |

| American-Style Puzzles | | Clues Solved |
|---|---|---|
| Monthly | *Games* magazine (two-star) | 95% |
| Weekly | *New York* magazine | 96% |
| Daily | *Chicago Tribune* | 96% |
| Sunday | *Detroit News* | 97% |
| Daily | *Dallas Morning News* | 100% |
| Daily | *San Francisco Chronicle* | 100% |
| Daily | *St. Louis Post-Dispatch* | 100% |

Of course, none of the above puzzles are in the same class with the so-called British or "cryptic" crosswords. Most famous of these is the notorious (London) *Sunday Times* crossword. Mechanically identical to American crosswords, British puzzles use oblique and intentionally misleading clues. The whole ethos is different. With a British puzzle, you have to sit and think about clues. You don't really do that with the American kind. British papers run contests to see who can solve a puzzle first. It takes days or weeks.

"Plant which enables one to read superficially before the intention is reversed": That's a *typical* clue for a British puzzle. British clues employ conventions that are second nature to aficionados but not to those raised on American puzzles only. A question mark after a clue is a nudge in the ribs telling you to look for an anagram, ambiguous word, or other tomfoolery. To make matters worse, the diagram is looser with fewer intersections. It is less likely that the verticals will solve a difficult horizontal, and vice versa.

Ergo, someone who has never worked a British puzzle is at a

considerable disadvantage. Editor Frank W. Lewis of *The Nation*'s very British-style puzzle sends a set of tips to perplexed readers who write in. So do the editors of *Games* magazine, which offers "cryptic crosswords" in addition to the regular fare. Lewis's hint sheet tells you, for instance, that "Featured like Goldilocks' villain" means BEARFACED and, even more horribly, the clue "Bur" is supposed to elicit RUBTHEWRONGWAY. "Clues are often only a suggestion to get you started on the right track—you must fill in the gaps of association," counsels Lewis. "For instance, if the clue 'Before fall' leads to the answer PRIDE, you can be grateful that the clue wasn't 'Summer?' which also goeth before a fall!"

We did not offer our panelists any advice on how to interpret British-style clues. As a result, some of our testers—educated people, really—disgraced themselves by failing to get a single word of some British puzzles.

Easiest was a hybrid, the London *Sunday Times* Concise Crossword. It looks like a cryptic puzzle, with an airy diagram and numbers of letters after each clue. Most of the clues are straightforward, American-style synonyms and definitions. There are enough trick clues, though, to make it more difficult than any of the American puzzles: 54 percent.

From there the field gets much tougher. Again, the fabled Sunday puzzle of the London *Times* came off no worse than the daily puzzle. The primary competitor to the *Times*'s puzzle is that of the (Manchester and London) *Guardian*. The solvers found the *Guardian*'s daily puzzle somewhat easier than the *Times*'s, completing just 4 percent of the clues.

**British-Style Puzzles**

| | | Clues Solved |
|---|---|---|
| Weekly | *The Nation* | 2% |
| Daily | (London) *Times* | 2% |
| Monthly | *Games* magazine (Cryptic) | 3% |
| Sunday | (London) *Times* | 3% |
| Daily | (Manchester) *Guardian* | 4% |
| Sunday | (London) *Times* (Concise) | 54% |

The battle for title of hardest crossword puzzle is a dead heat. The completion rates for *The Nation* and the London *Times* (daily) both rounded to 2 percent in the initial tests. *Games* magazine's Cryptic puzzle and the *Guardian* puzzle came very close.

In an attempt to break the near-tie, we got a second puzzle from each of the four publications and had the solvers try them. The tiebreaker did not change the rankings or the rounded percentages.

The verdict: The hardest regularly appearing crossword puzzle is either that of *The Nation* or that of the daily London *Times. The Nation*'s puzzle was marginally harder by our tests.

# TWENTY

# THE BEST AMERICAN TOURIST ATTRACTION

# ONCE THE ONLY

famous person's home every American could visit was the President's. Now, spurred by the success of Elvis Presley's Graceland, such luminaries as Dolly Parton, Lawrence Welk, Johnny Cash, and Roy Rogers have opened their most private possessions and even their residences to adoring fans. Which is most worth your vacation time? For our quick, reasonably objective rating, we estimated each famous person's recognizability on a scale where Elvis Presley equals 1. Then we multiplied that by the number of items represented on a checklist of 26: (a) gold or platinum records; (b) cars; (c) guns; (d) keys to the city; (e) preserved dead animals; (f) preserved dead *albino* animals; (g) bowling trophies; (h) objects emblematic of the celebrity but *much larger than normal;* (i) 3-D likenesses of Jesus; (j) things made by convicts; (k) diplomas conferring honorary doctorates; (l) Kentucky Colonel proclamations; (m) papal indulgences or blessings; (n) locks of hair or wigs; (o) wedding outfits; (p) bedrooms—either the celebrity's real bedroom or a simulacrum thereof; (q) bathrooms; (r) marked parking spaces for the celebrity or family somewhere you are sure to see them; (s) commemorative liquor decanters of the celebrity; (t) manuscripts on unusual media at hand (e.g., a song scrawled on a paper bag); (u) Nobel Prizes; (v) Grammy awards; (w) Emmys; (x) anything from Bob Hope; (y) plaster casts of parts of the celebrity's body; and finally, (z) family members, living or dead, and including the celebrity him- or herself, resident at the attraction or present there during visiting hours. Stuff on sale in the gift shop doesn't count.

Let's start with America's original historic home, Mount Vernon (George Washington Memorial Parkway, Mount Vernon, Va.). Washington himself complained about the rubberneckers but never turned anyone away. Now over a million people visit the place each year—about twice as many as Graceland gets. Between the house proper, the outbuildings, and the small museum of George and Martha's belongings, the visitor is allowed a respectful, occasionally revealing look at the first First Family. There are four of Washington's guns, the key to the Bastille presented to Washington by Lafayette (close enough to count as a key to the city), a stuffed deer's head in the overseer's quarters, one wig, and Martha's satin wedding slippers, all that remains of her wedding outfit. You get to traipse through seven bedrooms on the tour.

Congress once wanted George's body right under the dome of the capital and even built a crypt for it, but the family nixed that idea. The tomb at Mount Vernon contains the graves of George, Martha, and four relatives. All told, 7 of the 26 checklist categories are represented. The man who would not be a king is easily as famous as the King, so Washington rates a 1.00 on the Elvis scale of recognizability. Multiplying 7 by 1.00 gives a rating of 7.00—our estimate of how much the average American really wants to see Mount Vernon.

Lincoln's log cabin birthplace (U.S. 31E and State Route 61, south of Hodgenville, Ky.) is not half as good as it sounds. For one thing, Lincoln's family moved away when he was two and a half, so the adult Lincoln couldn't even remember this place. After Lincoln became famous, the cabin was carted off to fairs and centennials. It was returned to its original site in 1911, and *they're not entirely sure that this is the same cabin.* Genuine or not, it is protected for posterity by a marble-and-granite memorial. Since Honest Abe never lived here as an adult—three states and who knows how many towns claim him as a favorite son—Lincoln's belongings are scattered all over the country. The only thing here that counts on our checklist is one bedroom, the interior of the cabin.

The line for the free White House tour (East Gate, 1600 Pennsylvania Avenue, Washington, D.C.) will probably be the longest line you've ever been in for anything. After two or three hours in the Washington humidity, you're going to be in a bad mood and expect a damn good look at the Bushes and how they live. Though the tour snakes through eight flamboyantly decorated rooms, you leave knowing little more about George and Barbara than you did. You don't see their stereo, things their grandkids made, or the kind of cereal they eat. Nor do you see much memorabilia of former Presidents aside from safe, boring stuff like dessert services. The spoilsports are the National Park Service's low-keyed management and a succession of First Ladies who tossed out all the interesting junk. Teddy Roosevelt installed a small menagerie of stuffed animal heads in the State Dining Room but you won't see them. They got donated to the Smithsonian. The only items that count on our list are one larger-than-life object emblematic of the presidency (the giant bronze head of Lincoln), the Nobel Prize (Peace, 1906, awarded to Theodore Roosevelt), the parquet floor that the tour guide says Bob Hope stood on the last time he entertained there, and the First Family themselves, whom you probably won't see. Total: 4 items.

So much for the public sector. Privately operated attractions know that they have to offer a more intimate view of their subjects to survive in the marketplace. There are at least five museums devoted solely to Elvis Presley, all of which more or less want you to think that they are *the* Elvis museum. Elvis's Graceland (3717 Elvis Presley Boulevard, Memphis, Tenn.) is the most famous, but it must stand or fall on its merits.

Although Elvis is gone, Graceland is still a private residence. Elvis's aunt lives there. She's upstairs watching TV or something while you take the tour. At night they take down the velvet ropes and she has the run of the place. The Graceland tour is testimony to the lack of an aesthetic common ground. The decor, far ghastlier than the uninitiated can imagine, draws mundane approval from 99 percent of the other members of the tour group. "Looks like a good place to have coffee in the morning," one visitor said of the Jungle Room, an Afro-Polynesian pastiche for which Elvis picked out the furniture in just thirty minutes.

The psychology buff will find in Graceland many mementos of Elvis's erratic mental states. You can see the video cameras that a paranoid Elvis installed to check on visitors, and you can go inside the jet Elvis ordered flown to Denver to get peanut-butter sandwiches. Few of us indeed can hope to have *our* mood swings documented so conscientiously for future generations. Most revealing is a small collection of Elvis's books in the Elvis Up-Close Museum. Several conspiracy-theory tomes on the Kennedy assassination keep company with a copy of the *Physician's Desk Reference,* the standard illustrated guide to pills. If you ask what Elvis died of, you're told heart failure.

You don't see the bedroom where Elvis died, but you do see the racquetball court where he played his last sets. Elvis is buried in the garden out back, alongside several relatives disinterred from Memphis cemeteries with permission of local authorities. Graceland's trophy room displays 248 gold or platinum records, a number still growing with every passing year.

After seeing Graceland, you may wonder what's left to show in the other Elvis attractions. Have you forgotten Elvis's Beverly Hills period? The main rival showcase, Jimmy Velvet's Elvis Presley Museum (1520 Demonbreun Street, Nashville, Tenn.), proclaims itself quite simply "The World's Largest Collection." It is the flagship of a chain of Elvis museums that includes branches in Orlando, Honolulu, and Memphis. Furniture from Elvis's Beverly Hills home has been transported to Nashville and assembled into authentic period rooms. Pride of the collection is the RCA television set that an increasingly demented Elvis shot out one night at Graceland (the picture tube replaced, unfortunately, in the name of restoration). Run by a friend of Elvis's who really is named Jimmy Velvet, the museum also contains a number of signed documents attesting to the authenticity of the objects on display.

Regrettably, the numbers do not support the claims of superiority. Eight items on our list are represented at Graceland; just 4 at Velvet's museum. The Nashville museum has 5 gold records vs. 248 for Graceland, one car vs. five for Graceland, one gun to Graceland's ten. Graceland has five members of Elvis's family, living or dead, vs. *none* for Velvet.

The Roy Rogers and Dale Evans Museum (15650 Seneca Road, Victorville, Calif.) is famous for its stuffed Trigger, but it's the scope of the collection that keeps you coming back. Trigger, Buttermilk, and Bullet—Roy and Dale's horses and dog—are only two of over a hundred specimens of taxidermy. (It would be almost impossible to give a definitive count because some are made into rugs and leatherwork.) Best taxidermy exhibit: the baboons frozen eternally in "see no evil, hear no evil, speak no evil" poses. Nearly every animal on display was a co-star, a pet, or killed personally by Roy. There are two albinos, one of them Roy's former pet albino raccoon. It died of natural causes.

You don't bag a menagerie like that without firepower. One hundred and seventy-four guns—two captured from the Vietcong, though probably not by Roy—await your inspection. There are great big guns, teensy-weensy little guns, the guns Roy used in his movies, and the guns Roy used in his personal life. There are guns for sale in the gift shop.

The Roy Rogers and Dale Evans Museum also has more *random debris* than Graceland, the White House, or any other rival. Vitrines overflow with contents of wallets, purses, glove compartments, and relatives' houses; old watches; paperweights; cuff links; origami made from money; plaques—stuff too good to throw away, but where are you going to keep it? The transparent candy flake bowling ball with Trigger's picture in the middle is something you don't see every day. The memory of a dead daughter is invoked with a totemic collection of personal effects (a plush poodle, a report card, bongo drums, and a troll doll). There are autographed photographs of numerous celebrities, including Morey Amsterdam, Red Buttons, and all of the doomed space shuttle astronauts. There is one extremely large object (the statue of Trigger out front) and one bona fide 3-D Jesus plus a gimme for a crucifixion scene that uses the same Fresnel grating technology to change into a resurrection when you move your head. Although Roy and Dale don't actually live in the Western-fort-inspired compound, the guardhouse upstairs is Roy's personal office.

If you think everyone regards Liberace as a joke, you're wrong, and if you think that a Liberace museum could not fail to make some acknowledgment of his death from AIDS, you're wrong again. The Liberace Museum (1775 East Tropicana Avenue, Las Vegas, Nev.) and his Las Vegas home (not yet open) testify to America's continuing fascination with all things Liberace. The museum makes a game effort to act like a bigtime museum. Instead of paying admission, you make a tax-deductible donation to the Liberace Foundation for the Performing and Creative Arts. A library is not on the tour but is open, presumably, to qualified scholars.

If nothing else, the exhibits are sufficiently well removed from the workaday world to provoke the holiday seeker's sense of awe and disbelief. Every day hundreds of fans, mostly middle-aged women dragging husbands who really didn't want to come, gape admiringly at Liberace's red, white, and blue Bicentennial outfit—expensive to make and impossible to recoup the cost in resale. "The World's Biggest Rhinestone" sounds neat until you find out that a rhinestone is just a piece of ordinary glass cut in the shape of a diamond. You could have a bigger one made if you wanted it badly enough. Diplomas, graduation photos, and a gown attest to the fact that Liberace was a Doctor of Humane Letters (Alliance College) and a Doctor of Music (Combs College). Neither institution is well known.

You may think that indulgences for sins went out with the Middle Ages, but the museum has a certificate from the Holy Father granting Liberace indulgence for his sins and a papal blessing. Nearby are the gold-plated casts of Liberace's hands. No explanation is offered, and none is needed. One family member, a sister-in-law, runs the museum.

The Lawrence Welk Museum (8845 Lawrence Welk Drive, Escondido, Calif.) doubles as the lobby of what is just possibly the least avant-garde dinner theater in America. Theater and museum are the focal points of Lawrence Welk Village, an eerie, bunkerlike enclave where Welk's most loyal fans have come to spend their sunset years. Welk has a home here, too, but you don't get to see it and he doesn't live there full-time. The Lawrence Welk Museum displays dioramas depicting various stages of Welk's life and career. There is a giant champagne glass, a life-size statue of Welk, and two life-size cardboard cutouts of him. One of the cardboard Welks is perpetually on closed-circuit television so you can see how you would have looked had you been a guest on Welk's long since canceled ABC-TV show.

Loretta Lynn's Dude Ranch and Museum (off State Route 13, Hurricane Mills, Tenn.) is part of her estate. The tour includes not only the museum but the house where Loretta and her husband, Mooney, live. As at Graceland, the second floor is off-limits, but you get a peek at those two most intimate of rooms, a bedroom and a bathroom. Prominently featured in the den is a portrait of Loretta done by a fan behind bars. Loretta's twelve guns, most of them kept close at hand in a rifle cabinet, are the maximum for a female celebrity.

Barbara Mandrell Country (1510 Division Street, Nashville, Tenn.) is the classiest personal museum in Nashville. Although it does not neglect the other Mandrell sisters, you won't forget which Mandrell's museum it is. Exhibits include a 3-D Jesus (a stained wood bas-relief replica of *The Last Supper* made by a Taiwanese fan) and two things made by Mandrell fans paying their debt to society (a wood-carved portrait of Barbara from the Oregon State Penitentiary and an inscribed piece of the wall from the Missouri State Penitentiary). Barbara doesn't live here, but there are realistic re-creations of her bedroom and bathroom for the curious. More than any other, the Mandrell museum demonstrates the almost scary interlocking cabal of museum-worthy personalities. Mandrell Country has mementos from Elvis, Roy Rogers, and Lawrence Welk—all of whom are or were close personal friends.

Though patently a come-on to get you into the capacious Hank Williams Jr. Gift Shop, the Hank Williams Jr. Museum (1524 Demonbreun Street, Nashville, Tenn.) wins hands down for candor. Looping videos frankly discuss Hank Jr.'s chronic depression, his suicide attempt with Darvon, and both Hanks' alcoholism. Stranger yet, exhibit cases display Hank Sr.'s death certificate and two commemorative Jim Beam bourbon decanters. One is a musical statuette of Hank Jr. that plays "Family Tradition" as you pour yourself a good stiff one. Relatively austere with only two cars and six gold records, the museum is the beneficiary of Hank Jr.'s fascination with guns (eleven) and animals killed by them (four, one a lion).

"Nowhere else is a superstar so accessible," brags the brochure for Twitty City (1 Music Village Boulevard, Hendersonville, Tenn.), site of Conway Twitty's home and the world's first museum of Twitty memorabilia. You may not be all that clear on who Conway Twitty is, but he sure knows how to build a monument to his arguable fame. The museum has the best car yet, a vintage sea-foam-green T-bird with 61 miles on the odometer. Then the lights dim and the tour hostess bids you to contemplate Conway's Wall of Gold. A galaxy of twinkling blue lights swarms around 53 gold records as a light system casts whirling highlights on them. It is probably fair to say that most Americans have never heard of a *single one* of the records, but so what? *Somebody* bought them, or they wouldn't be gold records.

The fishbowl lifestyle reaches its apotheosis here as the tours tramp right through Conway's front yard for a good look at his house. Sometimes, according to guides, he waves to tours or comes out to sign autographs. That didn't happen the day we went. Nearby, Conway has built condo-style homes for his children and mother-in-law.

Ensconced on the grounds of Twitty City are several attractions devoted to lesser country and western stars. The most impressive is the Ferlin Husky Wings of a Dove Museum. Not sure who Ferlin Husky is? Posters and lobby cards remind you that he co-starred with Mamie Van Doren and Jayne Mansfield in *Las Vegas Hillbillys*. Wander into the back gallery for this museum's forte, religious dioramas and black-velvet paintings. There are thirteen 3-D Jesuses, a car, a "Reserved for Ferlin Husky" parking space out front, and ten gold records.

The Bill Monroe Bluegrass Hall of Fame is, despite the name, mainly a collection of other people's clothes. Skeeter Davis's perky gingham sundress is just one of the curatorial treasures here, possibly pending the establishment of a Skeeter Davis Museum. A Government Friends Wall honors politicians friendly to Bill Monroe and Bill Monroe-related interests—Ronald Reagan, for one. There's just one 3-D Jesus, but it's a good one. Turn your head and the image of Christ changes into a cross and praying hands. This is much like the picture in the Roy Rogers and Dale Evans Museum and shows the similarity of artistic tastes among the famous.

Across the road from Twitty City is the House of Cash (on State Route 31E, Hendersonville, Tenn.). Johnny's wife, June Carter Cash, is a Doctor of Humane Letters (National University, San Diego) ("Oh yeah, NU's Humane Letters program"). There are fourteen guns, the heads of two dead buffalo, one car (a Cadillac Johnny bought one piece at a time), and a whopping twenty-four gifts from convicts and prison guards, including a church made entirely out of gravel glued together. An irritable sign rebuts the rumor that Johnny was ever an inmate himself.

Dollywood (off U.S. 441, Pigeon Forge, Tenn.), a full-fledged theme park with rides, is home to a Dolly Parton Museum and a reconstruction of Dolly's humble childhood home. The collection is distinguished by a plaster cast of Dolly's foot. She used it to order custom-made shoes. Several of Dolly's less famous relatives work at the park.

By this accounting, Barbara Mandrell Country is the most complete attraction with 13 categories out of 26. But we'd estimate Mandrell's fame as no better than 0.20 on the Elvis scale. That means Mandrell Country's rating is 2.6.

The most revealing celebrity home is Graceland (8.0 rating), followed closely by Mount Vernon (7.0). Graceland has numerically more stuff than any place except the Roy Rogers and Dale Evans Museum, and people care about it more because it's Elvis's stuff.

# THE BEST AMERICAN TOURIST ATTRACTION

| | Gold or platinum records | Cars | Guns | Keys to the city | Dead animals | Albinos | Bowling Trophies | Extremely large objects | 3-D likenesses of Jesus | Things made by convicts | Honorary doctorates | Kentucky Colonel proclaimations | Papal indulgences or blessings |
|---|---|---|---|---|---|---|---|---|---|---|---|---|---|
| Graceland | 248 | 6 | 10 | 12 | 4 | | | | | | | | |
| Mount Vernon | | | 4 | 1 | 8 | | | | | | | | |
| Elvis Presley Museum | 5 | 1 | 1 | | | | | | | | | | |
| White House | | | | | | | | 1 | | | | | |
| Barbara Mandrell Country | 3 | 1 | 2 | 12 | | | | 1 | 1 | 2 | | | |
| Dollywood | 29 | | | 1 | | | | | | | | | |
| Roy Rogers and Dale Evans Museum | | 4 | 174 | 36 | 113 | 2 | 20 | 1 | 2 | | | 1 | |
| Liberace Museum | 3 | 7 | | 9 | | | | 1 | | | | | 2 |
| House of (Johnny) Cash | 35 | 1 | 14 | 7 | 2 | | | | | 24 | 1 | | |
| Lincoln's Birthplace | | | | | | | | | | | | | |
| Lawrence Welk Museum | 5 | | | 2 | | | | 1 | | | 1 | | |
| Hank Williams Jr. Museum | 6 | 2 | 11 | | 4 | | | 1 | | 1 | | | |

| Locks of hair | Wedding outfits | Bedrooms | Bathrooms | Marked parking spaces | Liquor decanters | Manuscripts in unusual media | Nobel Prizes | Grammys | Emmies | Anything from Bob Hope | Plaster casts of part of body | Members of family present | Categories represented | Fame | Rating |
|---|---|---|---|---|---|---|---|---|---|---|---|---|---|---|---|
| | 1 | | | | | | | 3 | | | | 5 | 8 | 1.00 | 8.00 |
| 1 | 1 | 7 | | | | | | | | | | 6 | 7 | 1.00 | 7.00 |
| | | 1 | | | | | | | | | | | 4 | 1.00 | 4.00 |
| | | | | | | | 1 | | | 1 | | 2 | 4 | 1.00 | 4.00 |
| 1 | 1 | 1 | 1 | | | 1 | | 2 | | | | | 13 | 0.20 | 2.60 |
| 2 | | 1 | | | | 4 | | 4 | | | 1 | 6 | 8 | 0.30 | 2.40 |
| | | | | | | | | | | 1 | | 1 | 11 | 0.20 | 2.20 |
| | | 1 | | | | | | | 2 | 1 | 2 | 1 | 10 | 0.20 | 2.00 |
| | 1 | 1 | | | | | | | | | | | 9 | 0.20 | 1.80 |
| | | 1 | | | | | | | | | | | 1 | 1.00 | 1.00 |
| | | | | | | | | | | | | | 4 | 0.20 | 0.80 |
| | 1 | | | | 2 | | | | | | | | 8 | 0.05 | 0.40 |

| | Gold or platinum records | Cars | Guns | Keys to the city | Dead animals | Albinos | Bowling Trophies | Extremely large objects | 3-D likenesses of Jesus | Things made by convicts | Honorary doctorates | Kentucky Colonel proclamations | Papal indulgences or blessings |
|---|---|---|---|---|---|---|---|---|---|---|---|---|---|
| Loretta Lynn's Dude Ranch and Museum | 7 | 2 | 12 | 12 | | | 1 | 1 | | 1 | | 2 | |
| (Conway) Twitty City | 53 | 1 | | | | | | | | | | | |
| Ferlin Husky Museum | 10 | 1 | | | | | | | 13 | | | | |
| Bill Monroe Bluegrass Hall of Fame | 2 | | | | | | | | 1 | | | | |

| Locks of hair | Wedding outfits | Bedrooms | Bathrooms | Marked parking spaces | Liquor decanters | Manuscripts in unusual media | Nobel Prizes | Grammys | Emmies | Anything from Bob Hope | Plaster casts of part of body | Members of family present | Categories represented | Fame | Rating |
|---|---|---|---|---|---|---|---|---|---|---|---|---|---|---|---|
|  |  | 1 | 1 |  |  |  |  |  |  |  |  | 2 | 11 | 0.03 | 0.33 |
|  |  |  |  |  |  |  |  | 1 |  |  |  | 7 | 4 | 0.02 | 0.08 |
|  |  |  |  | 1 |  |  |  |  |  |  |  |  | 4 | 0.02 | 0.08 |
|  |  |  |  | 1 |  |  |  |  |  |  |  |  | 3 | 0.001(?) | 0.003 |

# TWENTY - ONE

# THE MOST ACCURATE WEATHER- PREDICTING GROUNDHOG

# EACH YEAR

towns across America wage ugly smear campaigns to discredit each other's weather-predicting groundhog. One of the bitterest of American feuds pits Phil of Punxsutawney, Pa. ("The Weather Capital of World"), against rival hogs. Contenders include Woodrow K. Chuck IV, official groundhog of the state of New Jersey, who resides at the Turtle Back Zoo in South Orange; another Chuck (unrelated) at the Staten Island Zoo, official groundhog of New York; the Chicago Brookfield Zoo's Chipper; General Lee of Lilburn, Ga.; and Jimmy V, who shows up in the American Legion parking lot in Sun Prairie, Wisc. As the Roman numerals after the names attest, a seer's reign is short, and people have better things to do than think up names for animals that die so fast.

Sun Prairie's Jimmy is supposed to have been correct 23 out of 29 times in the period 1958 through 1987, while New Jersey's Woodrow K. Chuck is "better than the long range forecasts of the National Weather Service," according to a fawning 1980 write-up in the *Newark Star-Ledger*. Staten Island's Chuck modestly claims 85 percent accuracy, and suburban Atlanta's General Lee is said to be 7 for 8. Oh yeah? The burgers of Quarryville, Pa., claim pontiff-like infallibility for their Octorara Orphie. Punxsutawney Phil's people insist rabidly that he has never been wrong in 99 years. Not once! (The *Staten Island Advance* cited without attribution a 17 percent accuracy rate for Punxsutawney Phil—this in a 1984 puff piece on Chuck.) The rivalry periodically overflows into the halls of Congress, with congressmen from the states in question reading boasts and predictions into the *Congressional Record*. This delights the folks back home and is part of the reason why getting something in the *Congressional Record* doesn't mean a whole lot.

Things descended to a new level of unpleasantness in 1952, when a lax justice of the peace issued a marriage certificate to two Sun Prairie groundhogs in the hope that they would bear legitimate offspring and allow Wisconsinites to brand the Pennsylvania rodent a bastard. A weak joke to some of us, but good U.S. tax dollars paid to have these zany doings recorded at length in the *Congressional Record*. A hate-filled leaflet put out by the Sun Prairie Chamber of Commerce says, ". . . the shamelessly exaggerated claims of the weather-forecasting abilities of the Punxsutawney groundhog have been rightfully exposed. Contrary to reams of public relations propaganda and other hyperbole that continues to emanate from that eastern city, we believe that our own Jimmy has proven 'beyond the shadow of a doubt' that the Pennsylvania groundhog is nothing more than a cheap imitation attempting to ride the coattail of

Jimmy's success to universal fame and glory." But in an interview with the *Washington Post,* Jimmy booster Emden Schey of Sun Prairie allowed that "there's no jury. There's never been a knock-down-drag-out fight. It's never been resolved."

In view of the fact that no one actually believes in groundhogs as weather omens, isn't one prognosticating hog plenty? Who *is* the most accurate?

It is difficult to tally the record of individual groundhogs, since they don't last that long. The first year of the Punxsutawney ritual, they *ate* the groundhog. Consider the short and brutish lot of the groundhog as limned in Woodrow K. Chuck and his heirs and assigns. Chuck III was eased into early retirement in 1984 when he bit clean through a handler's protective glove. The replacement died of a heart attack, the main killer of captive groundhogs, so they reluctantly brought back the cantankerous Chuck III. By the next February 2, that groundhog was dead. "Chuck's body just wore out," Turtle Back Zoo director Richard Ryan explained. "This might have been complicated by liver failure."

In practice the hogs are more than willing to submerge their selves in the corporate persona. Woodrow K. Chuck I, II, III, and IV have all been females. Some groundhogs are known by an individual name as well as the assumed name. Handlers aren't always sure who's who. They all look alike, and they'd sooner bite a chunk out of your finger than look at you.

We therefore rated the groundhog dynasties existing at various zoos and woodsy locales. The major sponsoring organizations were asked to submit their records to an impartial jury and allow it to decide the best groundhog on the basis of National Weather Service records. The recent predictions, based on official records and contemporaneous newspaper accounts, go like this ("Did" means the groundhog saw its shadow):

| | Punxsutawney, Pa. | Sun Prairie, Wisc. | Chicago | Quarryville, Pa. | West Orange, N.J. | Staten Island, N.Y. | Lilburn, Ga. |
|---|---|---|---|---|---|---|---|
| 1989 | Did | Didn't | Didn't | | Did | Didn't | Didn't |
| 1988 | Didn't | | Did | | Did | Didn't | Didn't |
| 1987 | Did | Didn't | No show | Did | Didn't | No show | Didn't |
| 1986 | Didn't | Didn't | | | Did | Didn't | Didn't |
| 1985 | Did | Did | No show | Didn't | Didn't | Didn't | Didn't |
| 1984 | Did | Didn't | Did | | Did | Did | Didn't |
| 1983 | Did | Did | | | Didn't | Didn't | Didn't |
| 1982 | Did | Didn't | | Did | Did | Didn't | |
| 1981 | Did | | Did | | Did | | |
| 1980 | Did | | | | Did | | |
| 1979 | Did | | | | Did | | |
| 1978 | Did | | | | Indecisive | | |
| 1977 | Did | | Did | | Didn't | | |
| 1976 | Did | | Did | | Didn't | | |
| 1975 | Didn't | | | | | | |

Punxsutawney saw its shadow every year from 1887 to 1974 *except* as follows: didn't see shadow in 1890, 1934, 1950, 1970; probably didn't see shadow in 1902; partial shadow in 1942; no show in 1943; no record for 1889, 1891–97, and 1899.

Punxsutawney alone has a nearly complete record of predictions going back to 1887. A town like Chicago or New York can take its groundhogs or leave them. For Punxsutawney, groundhogs are pretty much it. The civic center has a life-size statue of Punxsutawney Phil by Jimilu Mason, a "noted sculptress and former Punxsutawney resident." Carnival in Rio has nothing on Punxsutawney on Groundhog Day. After trekking to Phil's den on Gobblers Knob for the forecast, local bigwigs man the telephone lines to get the word out, then celebrate at an always sold-out Groundhog Banquet. The younger generation crowns a Groundhog King and Queen to preside regally over the Groundhog Hop that evening at the high school.

The official record includes such trivia as the first year the groundhog appeared on *The Today Show* (1952) and accounts of such pathetic bids for topicality as Phil's post-Sputnik trip to the moon (1958). Certain entries record how dark the shadow was (1938 saw the "blackest shadow in history"). Sadly, the latter comment smacks of the crassest revisionism. The claimed "unusually dark shadow" of 1963 would have augured the record-breaking cold of February and March 1963, a period that averaged more than five degrees below normal at the National Weather Service's Pittsburgh station. *Would have,* that is, had someone noted anything different about the shadow. There was no mention of the shadow's darkness, unusual or otherwise, in the wire stories that year. Even more venal is a revised call for 1983. The press release says, "No shadow; peered over shadow at 7:29 A.M. but saw no shadow." In fact, the wire services had reported that Phil did see his shadow that year. The prediction was wrong.

Just because a town is sure its groundhog is the most accurate doesn't mean it actually has records. The Sun Prairie people sent a press release with a highlighted sentence: "Records of his predictions have been kept since 1958, and his forecasts have been correct 23 out of 29 times." A handwritten note in the margin admitted, "This is all we have." The Slumbering Groundhog Lodge, keeper of the Quarryville hog, conceded, "We do not have a total written record of our predictions, but for the last thirty years or so, we feel our Orphie has been correct just about every year." With much the same sense of rigor, the lodge counts among its members Winston Churchill, Charles Lindbergh, and Harry Truman, all of whom were voted in in absentia and none of whom actually made it out to Quarryville for Lodge Night.

Old wire service stories were used to fill in the historical record for these undocumented hogs. The table lists the official predictions as interpreted by the human sponsors *at the time,* including some questionable calls. Under slate-gray skies in 1981, some mockers quipped that Punxsutawney Phil's indistinct shadow was from the television lights. Phil's prediction was right that year, though. In 1983 the Turtle Back Zoo cheapened the whole institution by recognizing *two* groundhogs, one supposedly predicting six more weeks of winter and the other an early spring. Since it was an overcast day (the winter prediction was founded on the fact that one groundhog immediately returned to his burrow as if frightened by a shadow), the early spring prediction was judged the legitimate one.

If the groundhog sees his shadow, that means six more weeks of winter; if he doesn't, that means an early spring. The standard folklore ignores all sorts of problem cases. What if the groundhog refuses to come out of his burrow on a sunny day? The question is more than academic, for groundhogs sleep about twenty-two hours a day in winter and have no especial love of spectacle. In the past, when the groundhog didn't want to come out of its burrow, the Punxsutawney folks used a *stuffed* groundhog. The Sun Prairie faction once used a fur glove turned inside out, and the Turtle Back Zoo has used prairie dogs in a pinch. Most would agree that such substitutions are not going to hurt the accuracy of predictions.

However, the television age has prompted draconian solutions to the no-show problem. Jimmy is kept in a cage and toted to wherever the media want him to be. Chicago zoo officials corral their seers in a cardboard box. Phil now inhabits a futuristic burrow with electric heat. If he proves a little camera-shy, they can turn up the juice and sweat him out.

At best, "six more weeks of winter" is a vague prediction. Middle America's groundhog belt can usually count on several winter storms after February 2. Between those storms are stretches of springlike weather. "Oh yeah, here's the early spring the groundhog predicted." The Turtle Back Zoo claims their hog's prediction of six more weeks of winter one year was vindicated by a snowstorm *ten* weeks after Groundhog Day. The amazing thing is that Jimmy was so *astoundingly wrong* six times that the doting citizens of Sun Prairie couldn't cover for him.

From the overblown coverage, you'd think that the predictions are valid for the entire world. We took the more conservative position that predictions should at least apply to the immediate vicinity of the groundhog in question. Predictions should be reflected in National Weather Service records of average temperatures in the nearest large city. That would be Pittsburgh for Phil, Madison, Wisc., for Jimmy, Chicago for Chipper, Philadelphia for Octorara Orphie, and New York for the two Chucks. Although the groundhog's six-week prediction window is technically February 2 through March 16, Weather Service data on average temperatures is figured on a monthly basis. Average temperatures for February and March were used as the basis for comparison.

A prediction of "early spring" sounds like it means no more snow at all, people walking around in shirt sleeves on February 3. That is asking too much of a groundhog. A prediction of early spring was deemed correct if only the average temperature for that year's February and March was higher than the long-term average temperatures for those two months. Likewise, "six more weeks of winter" was read simply as colder-than-average temperatures. The scorecard, based on official and incontestable Weather Service records, reads:

| | Punxsutawney, Pa. | Sun Prairie, Wisc. | Chicago | Quarryville, Pa. | West Orange, N.J. | Staten Island, N.Y. | Lilburn, Ga. |
|---|---|---|---|---|---|---|---|
| 1989 | Right | Wrong | Wrong | | Wrong | Right | Right |
| 1988 | Wrong | | Right | | Wrong | Right | Right |
| 1987 | Wrong | Right | | Wrong | Right | | Right |
| 1986 | Right | Right | | | Wrong | Right | Right |
| 1985 | Right | Wrong | | Right | Right | Right | Right |
| 1984 | Right | Right | Wrong | | Wrong | Wrong | Right |
| 1983 | Wrong | Wrong | | | Right | Right | Wrong |
| 1982 | Right | Wrong | | Wrong | Wrong | Right | |
| 1981 | Right | | Wrong | | Wrong | | |
| 1980 | Right | | | | Right | | |
| 1979 | Right | | | | Right | | |
| 1978 | Right | | | | | | |
| 1977 | Right | | Wrong | | Right | | |
| 1976 | Wrong | | Wrong | | Right | | |
| 1975 | Wrong | | | | | | |

Punxsutawney was right 32 times and wrong 46 times in the period 1887–1974. The year 1902 was not counted because the average of the recorded temperatures for Pittsburgh in February and March was exactly average that year.

It isn't fair to compare a lucky guess or two against a long record of hits and misses. Of the groundhogs for which we could find at least five documented, unambiguous predictions, the winner is—a tie. Both Georgia's General Lee and Staten Island's Chuck were right 6 out of 7 years for which records exist (86 percent accuracy).

| | Accuracy | Years Tallied |
|---|---|---|
| Lilburn, Ga. | 86% | 7 |
| Staten Island, N.Y. | 86% | 7 |
| West Orange, N.J. | 54% | 16 |
| Punxsutawney, Pa. | 45% | 93 |
| Sun Prairie, Wisc. | 43% | 7 |
| Chicago | 17% | 6 |

General Lee lives in a miniature Southern mansion and used to have a wife named Scarlett. She died of a heart attack. Each year, General Lee is lured outside with a plate of grits and a nonalcoholic mint julep. Art Rilling, General Lee's handler at the Yellow River Wildlife Game Ranch, complained to the *Atlanta Constitution* that "the Pennsylvania method of groundhog watching—where the groundhog is torn rudely from his winter's nap—could hardly be called proper." The General is permitted to emerge from his antebellum dollhouse whenever he wants—*within reason.* If he's not out by 8:30, they apply pressure. The house's front door is on a spring so that it shuts behind him like a gopher trap.

Lately, General Lee has always predicted an early spring. Punxsutawney Phil usually predicts bad weather. This suggests that General Lee's advisers are merely looking to please the masses. General Lee's rosy predictions make good copy and draw visitors to an otherwise deserted wintertime animal park. As to his "accuracy," General Lee may just be riding out a greenhouse-effect warming jag in Atlanta's climate.

The equally accurate Staten Island Chuck handily merits his designation as New York's official groundhog. Most of Chuck's predictions suspiciously overlap General Lee's. Punxsutawney Phil's supposed phenomenal accuracy melts away under the most casual scrutiny. With a 45 percent accuracy over 93 callable predictions, he would have to be right the next nine years in a row to just achieve 50 percent accuracy. Much more damning is the 1 for 6 record in Chicago. Since even a coin toss would be correct 50 percent of the time, Chipper is a striking case of what parapsychologists call negative ESP. The Chicago zoo could save taxpayers untold dollars' worth of carrots and monkey chow by having Chipper humanely put to sleep—at no loss to meteorology.

# TWENTY - TWO

# THE MOST ACCURATE TABLOID NEWSPAPER

# CAN YOU BELIEVE

what you read in the newspaper? The acid test of journalist veracity is the *National Enquirer* and like supermarket tabloids. To rate their accuracy, we examined four issues of six tabloid newspapers in March 1988 and attempted to confirm or refute each and every feature story in them.

All the tabloids contain editorial material that is neither true nor false: jokes, cartoons, quotes, puzzles, advice columns, and such. All contain gossip columns of unattributed celebrity hearsay. It would be difficult to confirm or deny each short gossip item, so these columns were not included in the tabulation. Most tabloids contain a regular astrology or tarot column—not really "true," but even legitimate newspapers have astrology features. None of these features was used in determining a paper's reliability.

That left about 50 to 100 actual "news" stories per issue. A few stories appeared in more than one tabloid or in regular news media. These stories were assumed to be legitimate. A few innocuous photo features were accepted at face value as well. The other items were subjected to a fact check. Names, locations, and other details were noted. We attempted to get the phone numbers or addresses of the principals through directory assistance and to contact them to ask if the reported event really happened.

Wherever possible, the papers were given the benefit of the doubt. Many outrageous stories were attributed to an actual and sincere lunatic. If we could get that lunatic on the phone, fine. A few sources had beefs about the way the story was reported. That was okay as long as they agreed with the gist of the story. Headlines often promised more than the story itself delivered. Headlines were not counted against a paper unless the article failed to check out as well. The only stories that decremented a paper's reliability index were *complete and utter fabrications.*

It is difficult to prove that something *didn't* happen. It is all the more difficult when dates and places are omitted and specifics are few. A large share of *Weekly World News* stories are set in towns that do not appear in the index of the comprehensive edition of the *Times Atlas.* A disproportionately high share of suspicious stories are set in South America, Africa, or China, posing severe logistical and language problems for the would-be fact checker. A few stories gave no checkable specifics at all. In those cases where it appeared the story might conceivably be true, we wrote the bylined reporter care of the paper asking for further information.

If a story defied credibility to begin with, and was not carried by any other papers, we figured that it could fairly be deemed a fake provided one of the following conditions was met: (a) it was set in a town not listed in any of several large atlases; (b) none of the principal persons, businesses, or organizations named in the article were listed in the most recent editions of their city's phone books; (c) it contained no checkable specifics and the writer failed to respond to our requests for further information; or (d) we contacted someone in a position to know who said the story *didn't* happen.

Surprising as it may be to the casual observer, the yellower journals trade mostly in cheesy yet *factual* fluff and fillers. Added to this is a modicum of demimonde journalism (the *Weekly World News*'s running of the picture of Ted Bundy's body) and other coverage not generally considered worthy of space in regular newspapers. Of the six tabloids, four achieved an accuracy of 100 percent. Not one of their shamelessly sensationalized items seemed to be a total fake. The *National Enquirer*'s reporting is both gullible and irresponsible, but you can't doubt that the woman with the 200 cats exists. They've got a picture of her. The *Enquirer*'s main journalistic innovation is the article attributed to an unnamed source. The airing-of-dirty-laundry items on rocky celebrity marriages and substance-abuse problems quote shadowy "close friends" or "sources close to" so-and-so. In the *Enquirer,* such articles are plausible and likely true, the handiwork of the *Enquirer*'s well-paid network of informant camera operators, waiters, and gardeners.

Rated on a par with the *Enquirer* were the *Star, Globe,* and *National Examiner.* Of these, the reportage in the *Star* was possibly the most unexceptionable, if only because it favored tame service features.

|  | Reliability | Confirmed | Unconfirmable |
|---|---|---|---|
| *National Enquirer* | 100.0% | 196 | 0 |
| *Star* | 100.0% | 168 | 0 |
| *Globe* | 100.0% | 208 | 0 |
| *National Examiner* | 100.0% | 224 | 0 |
| *Weekly World News* | 95.8% | 384 | 17 |
| *Sun* | 91.9% | 238 | 21 |

The *Weekly World News* and the *Sun did* have fabricated stories. They had them in every issue. Both apparently pay someone to sit at a desk and make up stories.

The *Weekly World News,* the sole black-and-white paper, is mainly aimed at people not hip enough for the *Enquirer.* The "world" in the name is no glittering generality. Anytime, anywhere in the world, a criminal has part of his body amputated as punishment under Islamic law, the *News*'s international desk is on the story. Thought *cannibals* weren't much of a problem these days? Take off those rose-colored glasses, pal.

The *News* had 17 apparent fabrications out of a total of 384 stories in the four issues examined ("Cavemen looked like Elvis," "Love-starved orangutan goes ape for dwarf," "Baby born wearing 3,000-year-old anklet," etc., etc.). Many of these stories had the byline Henry Weber. Even the letters to the advice columnist, Dear Dottie, seemed made up. Countess Sophia

Sabak, the resident royal psychic, is not listed in *Debrett's Peerage*.

Whereas the *Weekly World News* is often tongue-in-cheek, the *Sun* is more for people who are actually mentally retarded. *Sun* readers are treated, for instance, to a color picture of the monster that one of the Bee Gees saw in his back yard. The *Sun* is almost brazen about its fakery. Invented names and details are recycled, resulting in curious synchronicity. Three extremely dubious *Sun* stories in four weeks concerned a person named Kyle. In one case the guy started the story with the name John and was later referred to as Kyle. (British bachelor Kyle McCumber proposed to a woman he met over the phone on a wrong number; Irish detective Kyle O'Grady investigated a bag lady who trained rats to steal for her; Australian teen Satanist John a.k.a. Kyle Quayle vanished in a puff of smoke.)

A story credited to Joe Frick about a homeless man described as a "48-year-old former carpenter" is followed in a couple of weeks by another Joe Frick byline about a homeless man in a completely different part of the world who is a "46-year-old former carpenter." (Things are tough all over.) The earlier ex-carpenter story ("Wino's dog finds $10,000 lottery ticket . . . but owner blows it & they're back on streets in 2 months," March 1, 1988, p. 27) had a photo of the guy, eating out of a pot and clutching a bottle, looking too much like a bum to be real. His dog had a collar and looked freshly bathed and brushed. A letter requesting more specifics brought a response from a *Sun* editorial assistant saying that the letter had been forwarded to Frick, a free-lancer. Frick did not respond. All told, the *Sun* had 21 unconfirmable stories out of 238, making it the least reliable of the major tabloids.